MW01490853

Cherry Delights

Edited by Annette Gohlke, FWN Food Editor

ecipes Screened by Janet Ballone, Associate Editor

Illustration/Layout Artist: Janet Kumbier

oduction: Sally Manich, Joan Sobczak, Sue Flower

Cover photography by Tim Jewett

Library of Congress Catalog Card Number: 82-50004
ISBN 0-89821-041-0
Copyright 1982 Reiman Publications, Inc.
Post Office Box 572
Milwaukee, Wisconsin 53201

Cherries...From Our Kitchen

Dear Friends:

We're so enthused about the recipes in this book, we're convinced you could make any of these recipes over and over and get no complaints from your family!

Even so, we hope you'll want to try *all kinds* of new and exciting cherry recipes now that you have this Farm Wife News cookbook. Instead of the usual cherry pie, why not put the delicious taste of cherries into pudding, a pretty salad, or cherry puffs?

Cherry Delights also has recipes for tarts and tortes, cobblers and crunches, or puddings and parfaits. There are recipes for muffins, breads and coffee cakes that would make perfect breakfast or snack-time treats, too.

Of course, no cherry cookbook would be complete without recipes for pies, cherry cakes and preserves. *Cherry Delights* has those and more—a wide selection of unique recipes with just the right ingredients to give "traditional" cherry delights brand new appeal.

Now that you have this book, you'll have recipes to use during cherry season and all year-round. You'll find recipes that call for fresh or frozen cherries, canned cherries or cherry pie filling.

On a day when you have time to spend in the kitchen, you might want to choose a recipe that starts from scratch with fresh cherries. But you'll also find a selection of recipes perfect to make on a busy day when you need a quick dessert for dinner.

Cherry Delights contains the very *best* recipes entered in our Farm Wife News cherry recipe contest. No matter which recipe you choose, we're sure your family or guests will tell you it was one of the best they've ever had!

Annette Gohlke

FWN Food Editor

Contents

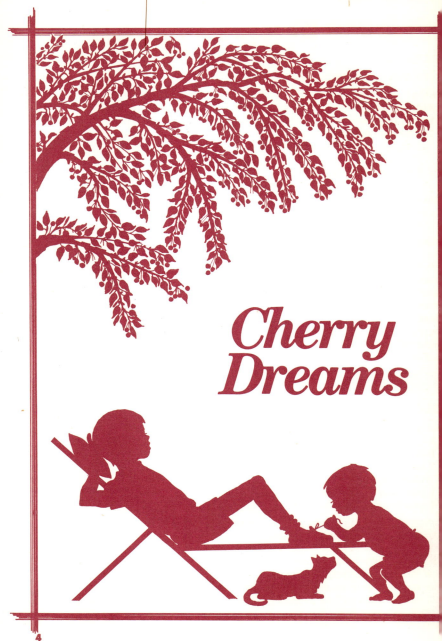

Cherry Dreams

Windowsill Pies

FRENCH CHERRY PIE

1 9-in. pie shell, baked

Filling:

3/4 cup sugar
1/3 cup cornstarch
1/8 teaspoon salt
1 cup boiling water
2 eggs
1 cup evaporated milk

1-1/2 teaspoons unflavored
   gelatin
1 tablespoon cold water
1/4 teaspoon almond extract
1 20-ounce can pitted, tart,
   red cherries, drained,
   reserving juice

Glaze:

1 tablespoon cornstarch
1/4 cup sugar

2/3 cup reserved cherry juice
1/4 teaspoon red food coloring

Filling: Blend sugar, cornstarch and salt in saucepan. Gradually add water, stirring to prevent lumping. Cook over medium heat, stirring constantly, until very thick. Remove from heat. Beat eggs; add evaporated milk. Slowly stir into sugar mixture. Soften gelatin in cold water; stir into sugar mixture. Cook, stirring, until mixture is smooth and thickened, about 5 minutes. Cool. Add almond extract. Turn into cooled pie shell. Spoon cherries over filling. **Glaze:** Blend cornstarch and sugar in saucepan. Slowly stir in reserved cherry juice. Cook over low heat, stirring constantly, until clear and slightly thickened. Remove from heat; blend in food coloring. Cool slightly before spooning over cherries. Chill pie a few hours before serving.

—**Cindy Kemp, Colome, South Dakota**

COLORFUL CHERRY-BERRY PIE

Pastry for double pie crust
3 cups sliced, peeled peaches
1 cup blueberries
1 cup halved, pitted, sweet
   cherries, fresh
1 tablespoon lemon juice
1/4 cup brown sugar

1/4 teaspoon allspice
1/2 cup granulated sugar
3 tablespoons flour
1/8 teaspoon salt
Milk
Sugared cinnamon

Combine peaches, blueberries and cherries. Sprinkle with lemon juice. Stir in brown sugar, allspice, granulated sugar, flour and salt. Mix gently. Line a 9-in. pie plate with half of rolled pastry. Trim overhang to 1 in. Spoon fruit mixture into shell. Cut remaining pastry into strips. Lattice strips over fruit. Tuck strips under edge of pastry. Make a rim; flute the edges. Brush with milk; sprinkle with sugared cinnamon. Bake at 450° for 10 minutes. Reduce heat to 350°. Bake 45 to 50 minutes more, until pastry is golden. Serve warm or cool. Serves 6 to 8.　　　　—**Cynthia Kannenberg, Brown Deer, Wisconsin**

CHERRY CREAM PIE

1 9-in. pie shell, baked

1 21-ounce can cherry pie filling

Filling:
2 cups milk, divided
1/3 cup sugar
3 tablespoons flour
2 tablespoons cornstarch
1/4 teaspoon salt

3 eggs, separated
1 tablespoon butter
1/2 teaspoon vanilla
1 tablespoon sugar

Meringue:
2 reserved egg whites
1/4 teaspoon cream of tartar

1/4 cup sugar
1/2 teaspoon vanilla

Filling: Bring 1-1/2 cups milk and 1/3 cup sugar to boil. Blend flour, cornstarch and salt with remaining 1/2 cup milk until smooth. Reduce heat to low; slowly stir flour mixture into hot, sweetened milk. Cook, stirring, until thickened. Beat 3 egg yolks slightly; stir into hot mixture; cook 1 minute. Stir in butter and vanilla; remove from heat. Beat 1 egg white with 1 tablespoon sugar until stiff. Fold into hot filling; chill. Spread cold filling over crust. Spoon cherries over top. **Meringue:** Beat 2 egg whites with cream of tartar to soft peaks. Gradually beat in sugar until stiff and glossy; add vanilla. Spread lightly over pie, sealing to edge of crust. Bake at 350° for 12 minutes. Chill at least 2 hours. **—Grace Baum, Bellevue, Ohio**

CHERRY ORANGE CHIFFON PIE

1 9-in. baked pastry shell, cooled
1 envelope unflavored gelatin
1/2 cup orange juice
1/2 teaspoon orange peel, grated

1 17-ounce can cherry pie filling, divided
2 egg whites
1/4 cup sugar
1/2 pint whipping cream, whipped

Soften gelatin in orange juice; dissolve over low heat. Add orange peel. Set aside 1/2 cup pie filling for garnish. Combine remaining pie filling and gelatin mixture. Chill, stirring occasionally, until partially set. Beat egg whites to soft peaks; gradually add sugar, beating until stiff peaks form. Fold in cherry mixture and whipped cream. Pile into pastry shell. Chill until firm. Garnish with reserved cherry filling before serving. Serves 6 to 8.
—Gertrude Fredrickson, St. Paul, Nebraska

LUSCIOUS MERINGUE PIE

4 egg whites
1 cup sugar
12 soda crackers or 18 Ritz crackers, coarsely crushed
1 teaspoon baking powder

1 teaspoon vanilla
1/2 cup chopped pecans
1 pint vanilla ice cream
1 21-ounce can cherry pie filling

Beat egg whites until stiff. Add sugar, 1 tablespoon at a time. Beat until stiff and glossy. Blend in cracker crumbs, baking powder, vanilla and nuts. Spread in lightly greased pie pan; bake 35 minutes at 300°. Cool. Fill with ice cream topped with cherry pie filling. **—Ruth Pool, Melvin, Illinois**

CHERRY CHIFFON PIE

Crust:

1-1/2 cups quick oatmeal, dry
1/2 cup chopped nuts
1/2 cup butter, melted
1/4 cup brown sugar, packed

Filling:

1 envelope unflavored gelatin
1/4 cup cold water
1 21-ounce can cherry pie filling
1/2 teaspoon almond extract
2 egg whites
1/3 cup sugar
1/2 pint heavy cream, whipped

Crust: Toast oatmeal and nuts in large, shallow pan at 350° for 12 minutes. Combine with butter and brown sugar; mix well. Press over bottom and up sides of greased, 9-in. pie plate; chill. **Filling:** Soften gelatin in cold water; stir over low heat to dissolve. Place pie filling in blender; chop for 5 seconds. Combine cherries, gelatin and almond extract in large bowl; chill until mixture thickens slightly. Beat egg whites until soft peaks form; gradually add sugar, beating until stiff and glossy. Fold egg meringue and whipped cream into cherry mixture. Pile into crust; chill about 3 hours. If filling is too much for 9-in. pie, spoon remainder into custard cups. A 13- x 9- x 2-in. baking dish may also be used. **Note:** Pie freezes well; thaw 1/2 hour before serving.
—Judith Voelker, Pierce, Nebraska

ANGEL CHERRY PIE

Meringue Shell:

4 egg whites
1/4 teaspoon cream of tartar
Pinch of salt
1 cup sugar

Filling:

4 egg yolks
3 tablespoons lemon juice
1 tablespoon lemon rind, grated
1/2 cup sugar
1/2 pint heavy cream, whipped
1 21-ounce can cherry pie filling

Meringue Shell: Beat egg whites until soft peaks form. Blend in cream of tartar and salt. Slowly add sugar, 2 tablespoons at a time, beating constantly until whites are stiff and glossy. Spread over bottom and sides of lightly greased, 9-in. pie plate. Bake at 275° for 1 hour. Turn off oven; let pie cool in oven. **Filling:** Cook egg yolks, lemon juice, rind and sugar in saucepan, stirring constantly, until thickened. Cool. Fold in whipped cream. Pile into cooled meringue shell. Top with cherry pie filling; chill.
—Joanne Vandeputte, Marshall, Minnesota

PATRIOT PIE

Crust:
- 1/2 cup lard
- 2-1/2 cups flour
- 3/4 teaspoon salt
- 1 egg, beaten
- 1 teaspoon white vinegar
- 1/3 cup cold water

Filling:
- 3 cups tart, red cherries, fresh, pitted (reserving juice)
- 1-1/2 cups sugar
- 3 tablespoons quick tapioca
- 1/2 teaspoon almond extract
- 1/4 teaspoon salt

Crust: Cut lard into flour and salt until crumbly. Add egg and vinegar to water; slowly add to flour mixture, mixing lightly with fork to moisten. Sprinkle with more water if necessary. Divide dough in half; roll out 1 piece to fit 9-in. pie plate. **Filling:** Mix cherries and juice with remaining filling ingredients; pour into prepared crust; dot with butter. Roll out remaining dough for top crust. Lattice over filling, or cut vents in closed crust. Seal and flute edge. Sprinkle with granulated sugar. Bake at 425° for 10 minutes, then at 350° for 45 minutes.   **—Florence Lorence, Racine, Wisconsin**

CHERRY PIZZA

Crust:
- 1 cup flour
- 1/4 cup confectioners' sugar
- 1/2 cup butter, softened

Topping:
- 1 8-ounce package cream cheese
- 1/2 cup sugar
- 1 21-ounce can cherry pie filling
- 1 8-ounce can chunk pineapple, drained
- Shredded coconut

Crust: Blend flour, powdered sugar and butter. Spread on greased pizza pan. Bake 12 minutes at 325° or until golden brown. Cool. **Topping:** Blend cream cheese and granulated sugar. Spread over crust. Top with cherry pie filling. Arrange pineapple over top. Sprinkle with coconut to give a real pizza look. Serve well chilled.   **—Peggy Miller, Topeka, Kansas**

HOMEMADE CHERRY PIE FILLING

- 4 cups cherries, canned or frozen
- 1 to 1-1/2 cups cherry juice
- 1 cup sugar
- 3 to 4 tablespoons cornstarch
- 1/2 teaspoon almond extract
- Few drops red food coloring

If frozen cherries are used, heat in saucepan just until juice flows as cherries thaw. Drain before cherries are warm. If cherries are sugared, reduce sugar to taste. Stir sugar and cornstarch together; add small amount of juice to make a paste. Stir into remaining juice; cook, stirring, until sauce thickens. Stir in drained cherries, extract and coloring; cool.

—Loraine Hurst, Milo, Iowa

Heritage Tarts

CHERRY KUCHEN RINGS

1 21-ounce can cherry pie filling

Dough:

1 package dry yeast	1 teaspoon salt
1/4 cup warm water	1 cup milk, scalded
1/4 cup sugar	1 egg
1/4 cup butter, melted	4 to 4-1/2 cups all-purpose flour

Topping:

1/3 cup sugar	3/4 cup light cream
1 tablespoon flour	1/4 teaspoon almond extract

Dough: Dissolve yeast in warm water. Set aside. Combine sugar, melted butter, salt and hot milk. Cool to lukewarm. Stir in unbeaten egg and yeast. Gradually add flour to form stiff dough. Knead on floured surface until smooth, about 5 minutes. Place in greased bowl. Cover with plastic. Let rise in warm place until light and doubled in size, about 1-1/2 hours. Roll out on floured surface to 15- x 12-in. rectangle. Cut into 20 rounds with 3-in. cookie cutter. Place on greased cookie sheets. Flatten to 1/4-in. thick. Roll out remaining dough to 1/8-in. thick. Cut into 1/4-in. strips about 5-in. long. Twist 2 strips together to form rings. Place on top of rounds. Press edges to seal. Fill center of each round with 1 tablespoon cherry pie filling. Cover. Let rise in warm place until light, about 45 minutes. Meanwhile, prepare topping. **Topping:** Combine sugar and flour in saucepan. Gradually add cream and almond extract. Cook over medium heat, stirring constantly, until mixture comes to boil. Cool. Bake rounds at 375° for 12 minutes. Spoon topping over filling; bake 3 to 5 minutes more, until golden brown. Brush with butter while still hot. **—Mrs. Milton L. Hanssen, Emery, South Dakota**

CHERRY CRESCENT TARTS

1 8-ounce can refrigerated crescent rolls	1/4 cup sour cream
	1/2 teaspoon almond extract
1 teaspoon butter, melted	1 21-ounce can cherry pie filling
2 tablespoons sugar	Slivered almonds
1 3-ounce package cream cheese	

Separate crescent rolls into 8 triangles. Press dough to cover bottoms and sides of 8 ungreased muffin cups. Brush dough with melted butter. Thoroughly combine sugar, cream cheese, sour cream and almond extract. Place 1 rounded tablespoonful in each muffin cup. Top each with scant 1/4 cup cherry pie filling. Sprinkle with almonds. Bake in 375° oven for 22 to 27 minutes. If desired, tarts may be served with whipped cream. Makes 8 tarts.
—Marjorie Crass, Medford, Wisconsin

CHERRY-ALMOND CLOUDS

Crust:

4 egg whites (room temperature)

3/4 teaspoon baking powder

1-1/4 cups sugar

1/2 teaspoon almond extract

15 saltine crackers, coarsely crushed

1/3 cup blanched almonds, chopped

Filling:

1/2 teaspoon almond extract

1 31-ounce can cherry pie filling

1/2 cup heavy cream, whipped

Crust: Beat egg whites and baking powder until soft peaks form. Gradually sprinkle in sugar, 2 tablespoons at a time, beating after each addition. Beat until mixture is stiff and glossy. Fold in 1/2 teaspoon almond extract, crushed crackers and almonds. Cover large cookie sheet with brown paper; spoon mixture onto paper in 8 mounds. Spread each mound to 4-1/2-in. circle, pulling sides up with back of spoon to form shells. Bake at 300° for 30 minutes or until done. Remove to rack; let cool. **Filling:** Add 1/2 teaspoon almond extract to cherry pie filling. Cover; chill. To serve, spoon cherry filling into shells; garnish with whipped cream. Serves 8.

—Teresa Egoian, Tulare, California

CHERRY FINGER PIES

Pastry for double pie crust

Filling:

1 16-ounce can pitted, tart, red cherries, drained

1/2 cup sugar

1 tablespoon quick tapioca

1/8 teaspoon salt

4 drops almond extract

Few drops red food coloring

1 tablespoon butter

Glaze:

1/2 cup confectioners' sugar, sifted

1 tablespoon water

1 drop vanilla

Filling: Combine cherries, sugar, tapioca and salt in medium saucepan; cook, stirring, over medium heat until mixture comes to boil. Simmer 5 minutes. Remove from heat; add almond extract, food coloring and butter. Cool. Divide pastry dough in half. Roll into two 12-in. squares. Cut each into four 6-in. squares. Put about 1/4 cup cherry filling in center of each square. Moisten edges, and fold each to form triangle. Seal edges by pressing with floured fork. Cut steam vents in top. Place on ungreased baking sheet. Bake at 425° for 12 to 15 minutes or until light brown. **Glaze:** Combine confectioners' sugar, water and vanilla. Brush over warm turnovers. Serves 8.

—Marlene Lehman, Shiloh, Ohio

CHERRY TRIANGLES

Filling:

3/4 cup sugar
5 tablespoons cornstarch
1/4 teaspoon salt
2 16-ounce cans water-packed tart, red, pitted cherries, drained, reserving juice

1 cup reserved cherry juice
1 tablespoon butter
2 teaspoons lemon juice
Few drops red food coloring

Dough:

2/3 cup milk, scalded
1 package active dry yeast OR
1 cake compressed yeast

1 cup butter
2-1/2 cups all-purpose flour, sifted
4 egg yolks, slightly beaten

Frosting:

1/4 cup butter
1/2 teaspoon vanilla
2 tablespoons cream

1-1/2 cups confectioners' sugar
3/4 cup chopped pecans

Filling: Mix sugar, cornstarch and salt in saucepan. Add cherry juice; cook, stirring constantly, until thickened. Stir in butter, lemon juice, cherries and food coloring. Cool. **Dough:** Cool milk to lukewarm; add yeast. Cut butter into flour. Add milk mixture and egg yolks; mix thoroughly. Turn out onto floured surface; knead about 10 times. Divide dough in half. Roll out first half until large enough to cover ungreased, 11-1/2- x 17-1/2-in. jelly roll pan. Spread cooled cherry filling over dough. Roll out second portion of dough. Place over cherries. Gently pinch edges of two dough layers together. Let rise in warm place for about 15 minutes. Bake at 350° for 45 to 55 minutes. Cool. **Frosting:** Cream butter, vanilla and cream. Add sugar, beating until mixture is well blended. Spread frosting over partially cooled pastry. Sprinkle with chopped nuts. When cool, cut into 3-in. squares; then cut each square in half diagonally. Makes 48 cherry triangles.

—Linda Barnes, Alexandria, Indiana

FINNISH CHRISTMAS TARTS

7/8 cup butter, softened
2 cups flour
1/2 cup water

1 teaspoon vinegar
Cherry preserves or jam
1 egg, beaten

Cut butter into flour with pastry blender. Add water and vinegar. Mix ingredients quickly to form dough. Do not knead too much. Add enough additional flour so dough isn't sticky. Refrigerate 2 to 3 hours or overnight. Roll to 1/8 in. thick. Cut into 5 or 6-in. circles. Fill circles with cherry preserves; fold over to form semicircles. Moisten edges; press together with floured fork. Brush with beaten egg before baking. Bake on ungreased cookie sheet at 400° for 15 to 20 minutes or until golden brown.

—Linda Barnes, Alexandria, Indiana

Presidential Tortes

FARINA CHERRY DELIGHT

6 eggs, separated
2 cups sugar
1/2 teaspoon salt
3/4 cup dry cream of wheat cereal
2 teaspoons baking powder

1 cup chopped nuts
1/2 cup dry bread crumbs
1 21-ounce can cherry pie filling
1-1/2 pints heavy cream, whipped

Beat yolks to light lemon color; beat in sugar and salt. Stir in cereal and baking powder by hand. Mixture is stiff. Stir in 2 unbeaten egg whites; add nuts and bread crumbs. Beat remaining egg whites until stiff; gradually fold into cereal mixture. Bake in greased 13- x 9- x 2-in. pan at 350° for 25 minutes or until done. Cool in pan; break cold cake into small pieces. Layer cake, pie filling and whipped cream in 3-quart, glass bowl, ending with cream. Refrigerate at least 8 hours. Garnish with cherry halves and nuts. Spoon into sherbet glasses. Serves 12.   **—Betty Secrest, St. Thomas, Pennsylvania**

HOLIDAY CHERRY TORTE

Crust:

1/2 cup graham cracker crumbs
1/2 cup flour

1/4 cup finely chopped walnuts
1/4 cup butter, melted

Filling:

2 tablespoons cornstarch
2 tablespoons poppy seeds
1 cup sugar
1/4 teaspoon salt
5 eggs, separated
1-1/2 cups milk
1 envelope unflavored gelatin

1/4 cup cold water
1 teaspoon vanilla
1/2 teaspoon cream of tartar
1/2 cup sugar
1/2 pint whipping cream
1 21-ounce can cherry pie filling

Crust: Combine crumbs, flour, walnuts and butter, mixing well. Pat onto bottom and sides of 8-in., springform pan. Bake 12 minutes at 325°. Cool. **Filling:** Combine cornstarch, poppy seeds, sugar and salt in double boiler top. Beat egg yolks; stir in milk. Slowly stir milk mixture into dry ingredients. Cook over simmering water about 10 minutes or until thickened, stirring constantly. Meanwhile, soften gelatin in water for 5 minutes. Add to hot custard; remove from heat. Cool; add vanilla. Beat egg whites and cream of tartar until frothy. Gradually add sugar, beating until soft peaks form. Fold custard into egg whites; pour into crust. Refrigerate overnight. Just before serving, whip the cream. Cover torte with cherry pie filling, and top with whipped cream.   **—Delores Hoefs, Pender, Nebraska**

CHERRY CHEESECAKE

Crust:

1 cup graham cracker crumbs
1/4 teaspoon cinnamon
1/4 teaspoon nutmeg

1 tablespoon sugar
3 tablespoons butter, melted

Filling:

5 eggs, separated
1 cup sugar
2 8-ounce packages cream
   cheese, softened

1 cup sour cream
2 tablespoons flour
1 teaspoon vanilla
1 21-ounce can cherry pie filling

Crust: Combine crumbs, cinnamon, nutmeg and sugar. Brush 9-in. spring-form pan with butter. Dust bottom and sides of pan with crumb mixture. **Filling:** Beat egg yolks until thick and lemon-colored. Gradually beat in sugar. Add cream cheese, beating until smooth. Blend in sour cream, flour and vanilla until smooth. Beat egg whites until stiff but not dry. Gently fold egg whites into cheese mixture. Pour filling into crust. Bake at 275° for 1 to 1-1/4 hours. Turn oven off; leave cheesecake in oven with door closed for 1 hour. Remove from oven; cool. Spread top with cherry pie filling.

—**Karen Bethel, Franklin, Kentucky**

BURIED TREASURE CHERRY CAKE

Crust:

1 3-ounce package cream
   cheese, softened
1/2 cup butter

1 cup flour
3 tablespoons sugar
1 21-ounce can cherry pie filling

Cake:

1/4 cup butter, melted
1/2 cup warm water
1 teaspoon vanilla
3 egg yolks, slightly beaten
1-1/2 cups flour
2 teaspoons baking powder

1/2 teaspoon salt
3 egg whites
1/2 cup sugar
Confectioners' sugar or whipped
   cream

Crust: Beat cream cheese and butter; add flour and sugar. Blend until dough forms; press onto bottom of 12- x 8- x 2-in. baking dish. Spread cherry pie filling over crust. **Cake:** Combine melted butter, water, vanilla and egg yolks; beat well. Add flour, baking powder and salt; beat until smooth. Beat egg whites to soft peaks; gradually add sugar, 1 tablespoon at a time, beating until stiff and glossy. Gently fold into yolk mixture until blended; spoon evenly over cherry filling. Bake at 350° for 45 minutes. Top with confectioners' sugar or whipped cream. —**Dena Fischer, Manchester, Iowa**

CHERRY BERRIES ON A CLOUD

Meringue:
- 6 egg whites
- 1/2 teaspoon cream of tartar
- 1/4 teaspoon salt
- 1-3/4 cups sugar

Filling:
- 1 6-ounce package cream cheese, softened
- 1 cup sugar
- 1 teaspoon vanilla
- 2 cups miniature marshmallows
- 2 cups whipping cream, whipped

Topping:
- 1 21-ounce can cherry pie filling
- 1 teaspoon lemon juice
- 2 cups sliced strawberries, fresh or frozen (thawed)

Meringue: Beat egg whites, cream of tartar and salt until frothy. Gradually add sugar, 2 tablespoons at a time, beating at high speed until meringue is very stiff and glossy, about 15 minutes. On piece of heavy, brown paper draw circle 10 to 11 in. in diameter. Place on cookie sheet. Pile meringue lightly inside circle, swirling and peaking to look pretty. Bake at 275º for 1 hour. Turn oven off, and leave meringue in oven to cool about 12 hours or overnight. **Filling:** Mix cream cheese, sugar and vanilla. Fold in marshmallows; gently fold in whipped cream. Peel meringue off paper; place on torte plate. Pile whipped cream filling lightly over meringue. Refrigerate 12 hours. **Topping:** Combine topping ingredients. (If using frozen berries, drain well.) Decorate top of filling with spoonfuls of topping. Pass remainder of topping in separate dish to spoon over individual servings. **Note:** Meringue may be spread in greased, 13- x 9-in. pan and baked but will not look as festive. **—Mrs. Howard R. Walker, Blue Mound, Kansas**

BLACK FOREST CHERRY TORTE

Cake:
- 2/3 cup butter, softened
- 1-3/4 cups sugar
- 2 eggs
- 1-1/2 teaspoons vanilla
- 2-3/4 cups all-purpose flour
- 2-1/2 teaspoons baking powder
- 1 teaspoon salt
- 1-1/4 cups milk

Filling:
- 2 tablespoons cornstarch
- 2 tablespoons sugar
- 1 16-ounce can pitted, dark, sweet cherries, drained, reserving juice
- 1 cup reserved cherry juice
- 1 tablespoon brandy flavoring

Topping:
- 1-1/2 cups whipping cream, chilled
- 1/4 cup confectioners' sugar
- 4 ounces sweet chocolate, grated

Cake: In large mixer bowl combine butter, sugar, eggs and vanilla until fluffy. Beat on high speed 5 minutes. Blend in flour, baking powder and salt alternately with milk, mixing on low speed. Pour into two greased and floured, 9-in., round pans. Bake at 350° for 30 minutes or until done. Cool 10 minutes; remove from pans. **Filling:** Mix cornstarch and sugar in 1-quart saucepan. Stir in cherry liquid. Cook, stirring constantly, until mixture thickens and boils; boil and stir 1 minute. Cool to lukewarm. Add brandy flavoring. Dip 36 cherries into filling; reserve coated cherries for top of cake. Cut remaining cherries into fourths; stir into filling. Thoroughly chill filling and dipped cherries. **Topping:** Beat whipping cream and confectioners' sugar in chilled bowl until very stiff. Place 1 layer of cake top side down on serving plate. Make rim of whipped cream around edge of cake. Fill center with all of cherry filling. Place second layer top side up over filling. Gently spread whipped cream on side and top of cake. Press chocolate onto side. Pipe border of whipped cream around top edge. Outline individual portions in spoke design on top of cake. Place reserved cherries in each portion. Store in refrigerator.   **—Karen Luebke, Garretson, South Dakota**

ALMOND-CRANCHERRY DESSERT

Crust:

2-1/2 cups sliced almonds, toasted, divided
  1/4 cup butter, melted

1/4 cup confectioners' sugar
1 teaspoon orange peel, grated
3/4 teaspoon cinnamon

Filling:

  2 3-ounce packages cream cheese, softened
  3 tablespoons plain yogurt

3 tablespoons confectioners' sugar

Topping:

  1 21-ounce can cherry pie filling
  1 8-ounce can whole cranberry sauce

3 tablespoons sugar
1 teaspoon lemon juice
1 teaspoon unflavored gelatin

Crust: Set aside 1/4 cup almonds for garnish. Finely grind remaining almonds in blender or food processor. Combine with melted butter, powdered sugar, orange peel and cinnamon. Pat mixture onto bottom and sides of 9-in. pie plate. Bake at 350° for 10 to 12 minutes or until lightly browned. Cool. **Filling:** Blend cream cheese, yogurt and powdered sugar together. Spread over cooled crust. **Topping:** In medium saucepan combine pie filling, cranberry sauce, sugar, lemon juice and gelatin. Heat just to boiling, stirring constantly. Chill just until mixture begins to thicken. Spoon topping over cheese filling. Chill until firm, about 6 hours. Sprinkle with remaining almonds, leaving 1-in. border around edge. Serves 8.
—Laurie Pronschinske, Arcadia, Wisconsin

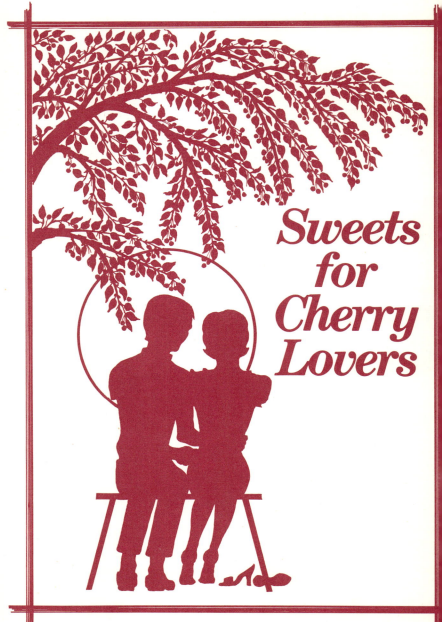

Sweets for Cherry Lovers

Ice Cream Parlor Treats

QUICK CHERRY PARFAIT

1 cup milk
1 cup dairy sour cream
1 teaspoon almond extract

1 3-1/2-ounce package instant
   vanilla pudding mix
1 21-ounce can cherry pie filling
1/4 cup slivered almonds, toasted

Combine milk, sour cream, almond extract and pudding mix. Beat until creamy, about 2 minutes. Layer pudding mixture and cherries in parfait glasses. Top layer should be cherries. Sprinkle with almonds. Serves 6.

—Lela E. Steiner, Pandora, Ohio

CHERRY SHAKE

1 cup tart, pitted, red cherries,
   fresh or frozen
1/4 cup sugar

2 cups milk
1 pint vanilla ice cream

In blender thoroughly combine cherries and sugar. Add milk; blend again. Add ice cream; blend until smooth. Pour into insulated mugs. Serves 4. **Note:** Add 1/4 cup malted milk powder if a malt is desired.

—Dorothy Dadisman, Nevada, Iowa

SWEET CHERRY SODA

1-1/2 cups sweet, pitted cherries
1/3 cup sugar
Vanilla ice cream

Cherry-flavored carbonated
   beverage

Chill two 12-ounce glasses. Combine cherries and sugar in blender. Add large scoop of ice cream; blend well. Pour mixture into glasses; fill with carbonated cherry beverage.   —Mrs. Ellison E. Austin, Clarkston, Michigan

---

SO EASY CHERRIES JUBILEE

2 sugar cubes
Lemon extract
1 10-ounce jar red currant jelly

2 16-ounce cans pitted, dark,
   sweet cherries, drained
1 quart vanilla ice cream

About 24 hours before serving, soak sugar cubes in lemon extract. Next day, heat jelly until melted. Add cherries; heat until cherries and jelly simmer. Scoop ice cream into sherbet glasses; spoon hot cherry sauce over ice cream. Place 1 sugar cube on top of ice cream. Light with match; serve flaming. Extinguish; remove sugar cube before eating. Serves 12.

—Virginia Claypool, Marshall, Illinois

Liberty Puddings

DUTCH CHERRY PUDDING

Pudding:
- 1 cup all-purpose flour, sifted
- 1-1/2 teaspoons baking powder
- 1/2 teaspoon salt
- 2 tablespoons sugar
- 1/4 cup shortening
- 1 egg
- 1/4 cup milk
- 1/2 teaspoon vanilla
- 1/4 teaspoon almond extract
- 1 20-ounce can red, tart, pitted cherries, drained, reserving juice

Topping:
- 2 egg yolks
- 1/2 cup sugar
- 1 cup sour cream

Sauce:
- 1 cup reserved cherry juice
- 2 tablespoons flour
- 1/2 cup sugar
- 1/2 tablespoon butter
- 2 drops red food coloring, optional
- 1/2 pint whipping cream, whipped

Pudding: Sift flour, baking powder, salt and sugar together. Cut in shortening until crumbs form. Add egg, milk and flavorings; beat 150 strokes. Spread in greased, 8-in. square pan. Arrange cherries on top of pudding. **Topping:** Beat egg yolks until light. Add sugar and sour cream; mix well. Pour over cherries. Bake at 400° for 45 to 55 minutes, until topping is browned. **Sauce:** Bring cherry liquid to boil. Mix flour and sugar; add to cherry juice. Boil until thickened, about 5 minutes. Remove from heat; add butter and food coloring. Cool. Serve over warm pudding. Top with whipped cream.
—Gladys Parmenter, Austin, Minnesota

CHERRY DUMP PUDDING

- 1 cup flour
- 1/4 teaspoon salt
- 1 teaspoon baking powder
- 1/2 cup sugar
- 1/4 cup shortening
- 1/2 cup milk
- 1 teaspoon vanilla
- 2 cups pitted, tart, red cherries, drained, reserving juice
- 1/2 to 3/4 cup sugar
- 1 cup reserved cherry juice

Sift together flour, salt, baking powder and 1/2 cup sugar. Add shortening, milk and vanilla. Beat vigorously with spoon or electric mixer about 2 minutes. Pour into greased, 10- x 6-in. pan. Cover with cherries. Sprinkle with 1/2 to 3/4 cup sugar. Pour boiling hot cherry liquid over cherries. Bake at 350° about 50 minutes. Serve warm with cream, whipped cream or ice cream. Serves 6 to 8.
—Mary Schmidt, Mt. Hope, Kansas

OLD-FASHIONED CHERRY PUDDING

Pudding:

1 cup sugar
1/4 teaspoon baking soda
1 tablespoon butter

2 cups flour
1 cup sour milk

Topping:

1 cup tart, pitted, red cherries,
    fresh or frozen (thawed)
1 cup sugar

2 tablespoons butter
1 cup boiling water

Pudding: Stir together sugar, baking soda, butter, flour and sour milk until well blended. Pour into greased, 9-in. square baking dish. **Filling:** Combine cherries, sugar and butter. Spread over batter. Pour boiling water over top. Bake at 375° for 35 minutes. Serve warm with ice cream or cold with whipped cream. **—Lavonda Martin, Alto, Michigan**

CHERRY CHEESE MOUSSE

1-1/2 teaspoons unflavored gelatin
1 cup pineapple juice
1/2 cup sugar
1 tablespoon lemon juice
2 3-ounce packages cream
    cheese, softened

1/2 teaspoon almond extract
1/8 teaspoon salt
1/2 cup heavy cream, whipped
1 cup pitted, dark, sweet
    cherries, sliced
Additional cherries for garnish

Sprinkle gelatin on pineapple juice in saucepan. Stir in sugar; heat, stirring, until gelatin and sugar are dissolved. Cool. Add lemon juice. Blend cream cheese with almond extract and salt; beat until fluffy. Gradually beat in gelatin mixture. Fold in whipped cream and sliced cherries. Turn into 1-quart mold. Freeze several hours or overnight. Unmold. Garnish with whole cherries. Serves 6. **—Mrs. J.F. Finnegan, Minneota, Minnesota**

MOUNT VERNON CHERRY-BERRY PUDDING

1 16-ounce can dark, pitted
    sweet cherries
2 10-ounce packages frozen,
    sliced strawberries, thawed

3 tablespoons instant tapioca
1/4 teaspoon salt
1/2 pint whipping cream, whipped

Drain cherries and strawberries, reserving liquids. Combine liquids with enough water to equal 2-1/2 cups. In saucepan combine juice, tapioca and salt; bring to boil over medium heat, stirring occasionally. Remove from heat; stir in cherries and strawberries. Cool 15 minutes; stir to mix well. Refrigerate uncovered until well chilled. To serve, spoon into stemmed glasses. Garnish with whipped cream. Serves 6.

—Teresa Egoian, Tulare, California

CHERRY CHARLOTTE RUSSE

1 envelope unflavored gelatin
1 16-ounce can sweet, pitted,
 dark cherries, drained,
 reserving juice
1-1/2 cups reserved cherry juice
 plus water
1 3-ounce package cherry
 gelatin

1/4 cup sugar
1 cup plain yogurt
1 cup whipping cream, whipped
1 cup orange sections, cut up
1/4 cup slivered almonds, toasted
1 bakery jelly roll, cut into
 1/2-in. slices

Soften unflavored gelatin in cherry liquid. Heat to boiling, stirring occasionally. Add cherry gelatin and sugar; stir to dissolve. Pour into large mixing bowl; chill until very thick. Beat until fluffy, gradually adding yogurt. Fold in whipped cream, cherries, oranges and almonds. Arrange jelly roll slices around sides of 9-in., springform pan. Spoon gelatin mixture into pan; chill until firm.   **—Mrs. Webster Orton, Algona, Iowa**

Old-Fashioned Fruit Soups

CHERRY FRUIT SOUP

1 16-ounce can water-packed,
 pitted, tart, red cherries
1/2 cup sugar
1 orange, sliced
1 2-in. stick cinnamon

6 whole cloves
1 teaspoon lemon juice
1 16-ounce can sliced peaches,
 drained, reserving syrup
2 teaspoons cornstarch

Combine cherries and juice with sugar, orange, cinnamon, cloves and lemon juice in 1-1/2-quart saucepan. Add a little peach syrup to cornstarch; add remainder to cherry mixture. Cook cherry mixture over low heat, stirring constantly. Stir in thickened peach syrup; continue to cook, stirring, until thickened. Add peaches. Serve warm or cold. Serves 6.

—Dora Rupnow, Jefferson, Wisconsin

GINGER-SPICED CHERRIES

2 1-pound cans pitted, dark,
 sweet cherries, drained
 reserving juice
2 tablespoons cornstarch
1-1/2 tablespoons lemon juice

1/4 cup sugar
Pinch salt
 2 tablespoons candied ginger,
 thinly sliced

Mix small amount of cherry juice with cornstarch to form a paste. Add remaining cherry juice, lemon, sugar, salt and ginger. Cook until clear and thickened; add cherries. Serve cold. **—Debra Frisco, Rochester, Vermont**

FRESH CHERRY SOUP

1 cup fresh orange juice
1 cup pineapple juice
2 cups buttermilk
2 cups sour cream
6 tablespoons honey
2 tablespoons fresh lemon juice

2 teaspoons ground cinnamon
1 teaspoon freshly ground nutmeg
2 pints red, tart cherries, fresh
Fresh mint leaves for garnish,
    optional

In large bowl, combine orange and pineapple juices, buttermilk, sour cream, honey, lemon juice, cinnamon and nutmeg to taste. Beat until well blended. Set aside. Wash, drain and pit cherries, leaving cherries whole. Add to soup mixture. Cover and refrigerate until thoroughly chilled, at least 4 hours. Garnish with mint leaves if desired. Serves 8.

—Angel Janssen (Thimbleberry Inn), Egg Harbor, Wisconsin

RUBY FRUIT COMPOTE

2 cups pitted, tart, red cherries,
    drained, reserving juice
1 10-ounce package
    raspberries, frozen (thawed
    and drained, reserving juice)
Sour cream

2 cups combined cherry and
    raspberry liquid
1-1/2 tablespoons cornstarch
1 tablespoon lemon juice
2 cups strawberries, fresh

Add small amount of combined cherry and raspberry juice to cornstarch, stirring to a paste. Heat fruit juices until warm; add cornstarch paste. Cook, stirring constantly, until thickened and bubbling; cook 1 minute more. Remove from heat; add lemon juice. Combine cherries, raspberries and strawberries. Pour hot sauce over fruit, mixing gently. Cover; chill. Top with dollop of sour cream.   —Cleone Doggett, Oakes, North Dakota

---

DANISH CHERRY FRUIT SOUP

1/2 cup pearl tapioca
1 quart water
1 12-ounce package pitted prunes
1 pound seedless raisins

1 cup dried apricots
1 stick cinnamon
24 ounces white grape juice
1 21-ounce can cherry pie filling

Soak pearl tapioca in water overnight in large saucepan. Next morning, add prunes, raisins, dried apricots and cinnamon stick. Bring to boil, stirring several times so fruit doesn't stick to pan. Reduce heat to low; simmer until fruit is tender. As mixture thickens, gradually stir in white grape juice. Remove cinnamon stick; cool to lukewarm. Add cherry pie filling. Serve warm, cold or at room temperature. Keeps well refrigerated.

—Gloria Kratz, Des Moines, Iowa

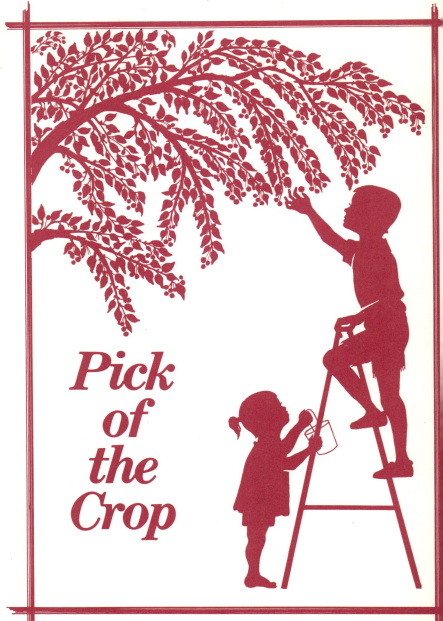

Pick
of
the
Crop

Towne Squares

CHERRY MERINGUE BARS

Crust:
1/2 cup butter
1/2 cup confectioners' sugar
1 cup flour, sifted
2 egg yolks

Filling:
2/3 cup sugar
2-1/2 tablespoons cornstarch
1 16-ounce can pitted, red, tart cherries, drained, reserving juice
3/4 cup reserved cherry juice
1 tablespoon lemon juice

Meringue:
2 egg whites
1/2 cup sugar
Slivered almonds, optional

Crust: Cream butter and confectioners' sugar; blend in flour and egg yolks. Press onto bottom of 13- x 9-in. pan. Bake for 18 minutes at 350⁰. **Filling:** Combine sugar and cornstarch; stir in cherry juice and lemon juice. Heat, stirring constantly, until mixture is clear and thickened. Add cherries. Remove from heat; cool. **Meringue:** Beat egg whites until fluffy; gradually add sugar. Beat until stiff. Spread cooled cherry mixture over crust; top with meringue. Sprinkle with almonds if desired. Bake at 350⁰ for 10 to 20 minutes, until meringue is lightly browned. Cut into bars.

—Barbara Shaw, West Bend, Wisconsin

GLAZED CHERRY BARS

Bars:
3/4 cup butter
1-1/2 cups brown sugar
3 eggs
2 teaspoons vanilla
2 cups flour
2 teaspoons baking powder
1/2 teaspoon salt
1/2 cup chopped walnuts
1 cup pitted, dark, sweet cherries, quartered

Glaze:
1 cup semi-sweet chocolate chips
1/2 cup peanut butter

Bars: Cream butter and sugar until fluffy. Add eggs and vanilla; beat well. Sift together flour, baking powder and salt; add to creamed mixture. Fold in nuts and cherries. Bake 15 to 20 minutes at 375⁰ in 13- x 9-in. pan. Cool. **Glaze:** Melt chocolate chips; blend in peanut butter. When bars are cool, frost with glaze.

—Janet Stengel, Milbank, South Dakota

CHERRY TOASTIES

Squares:

1 cup flaked coconut
1/2 cup slivered almonds,
   coarsely chopped
1-1/2 cups crisp rice cereal

1/4 cup light brown sugar, firmly
   packed
1/4 cup butter, melted
1-1/2 quarts vanilla ice cream,
   slightly softened

Topping:

1/4 cup sugar
1 tablespoon cornstarch
1 20-ounce can frozen cherries,
   thawed, drained, reserving
   juice

3/4 cup reserved cherry juice
1/8 teaspoon red food coloring
1 tablespoon lemon juice
1 teaspoon butter

Squares: Toast coconut and almonds in 350º oven. Combine cereal and sugar with toasted coconut and almonds. Add melted butter; mix lightly. Pat half of mixture into greased, 8-in. square pan. Spread evenly with ice cream. Spread remaining cereal mixture over top. Chill in freezer. **Topping:** Combine sugar, cornstarch, cherry juice and food coloring in saucepan. Cook until mixture is thickened, stirring constantly. Remove from heat; add lemon juice, butter and cherries. Cool. Serve topping over chilled squares.

—Wanda Koepke, Milbank, South Dakota

CHERRY-NUT TREATS

1 cup butter
2 cups sugar
1 teaspoon vanilla
3 eggs, beaten
1/4 teaspoon almond extract
1 cup flour, sifted

1/2 teaspoon salt
1/2 teaspoon cinnamon
1 cup fresh cherries, halved,
   pitted
1/2 cup flaked coconut
1 cup chopped walnuts

Cream butter and sugar; blend in vanilla, eggs and almond flavoring. Add flour, salt and cinnamon; mix well. Stir in cherries, coconut and nuts. Spread in 13- x 9- x 2-in., greased pan. Bake 45 minutes at 350º. Cool 15 minutes; cut into squares.
—Lynda Paxton, Halethorpe, Maryland

CHOCOLATE-CHERRY BARS

Bars:

1 package devil's food cake mix
1 21-ounce can cherry pie filling

1 teaspoon almond extract
2 eggs, well beaten

Frosting:

1 cup sugar
5 tablespoons butter

1/3 cup milk
1 cup chocolate chips

Bars: Thoroughly combine cake mix, pie filling, extract and eggs. Pour into greased, 15- x 10-in. jelly roll pan. Bake at 350° for 20 to 30 minutes. **Frosting:** Combine sugar, butter and milk in saucepan. Boil for 1 minute. Remove from heat. Add chocolate chips; stir until smooth. Pour over warm bars. Cool before cutting. **Note:** Instead of frosting, bars may be served with ice cream or dessert toppings. **—Mrs. Lawrence Hanson, Souris, North Dakota**

Quick Cobblers 'n' Crunches

CHERRY CRUNCH

Crust:
3/4 cup butter
40 graham crackers, rolled fine

3/4 cup sugar
1 teaspoon cinnamon

Filling:
1-3/4 cups sugar, divided
5 tablespoons cornstarch
1 quart cherries

Few drops red food coloring
5 egg whites

Crust: Melt butter; mix with crumbs, sugar and cinnamon. Pat 3/4 of mixture onto bottom and sides of 13- x 9-in., greased pan. **Filling:** Cook 1-1/2 cups sugar, cornstarch and cherries until thickened and clear, stirring constantly. Add food coloring. Pour over crust. Beat egg whites until stiff; add remaining 1/4 cup sugar. Beat until stiff and glossy. Spread over cherries; cover with remaining crumb mixture. Bake 30 minutes or until golden brown at 350°. Cut into squares; serve plain or with whipped cream.

—Marilyn Schmidt, Buhl, Idaho

GRAHAM-MALLOW TREAT

Crust:
1-1/3 cups graham cracker crumbs
1/2 cup butter, melted

1/3 cup sugar

Filling:
1/2 1-pound bag large
　　marshmallows
1/2 cup milk

1 cup whipping cream, whipped
1 21-ounce can cherry pie filling

Crust: Mix crackers, butter and sugar together. Press into 12- x 8-in. pan, reserving 1/2 cup for topping. Bake at 350° for 8 to 10 minutes. **Filling:** Combine marshmallows and milk; melt over low heat, stirring constantly. Remove from heat, stirring occasionally as mixture cools. Fold in whipped cream. Pour 1/2 of marshmallow mixture over crust. Spoon cherry pie filling over top. Cover with remaining marshmallow mixture. Sprinkle with 1/2 cup reserved crumbs. Refrigerate.

—Judy VanDykhorst, Castlewood, South Dakota

POLKA DOT CRUNCH

4 cups pared, thinly sliced apples
1 17-ounce can tart, red, pitted
   cherries, drained
1 teaspoon cinnamon
1/2 cup sugar

5 tablespoons butter, divided
1 cup brown sugar
1/2 cup flour
1/4 teaspoon salt
1/2 cup grapenuts cereal

Put apples in well greased, 9-in. square baking dish. Spoon cherries over top. Mix cinnamon and sugar; sprinkle over fruit. Dot with 1 tablespoon butter. Combine brown sugar, flour, salt and 4 tablespoons remaining butter. Mix well with fork; blend in grapenuts. Spread evenly over fruit. Cover with foil; bake at 350° for 30 minutes. Bake uncovered 15 minutes more. Serve with ice cream, whipped cream or cherry juice thickened with 1 tablespoon cornstarch and 1/2 cup sugar for 1 cup juice.

—Phyllis Clinehens, Maplewood, Ohio

CHERRY CINNAMON COBBLER

Filling:

1/2 cup sugar
3 tablespoons red-hot
   cinnamon candies
2 tablespoons cornstarch

1/2 cup water
1 20-ounce can tart, pitted, red
   cherries, drained, reserving
   juice

Rounds:

1-1/2 cups flour
2 teaspoons baking powder
1/2 teaspoon salt
6 tablespoons brown sugar,
   divided
1/3 cup ground pecans, optional

1/2 cup shortening
1 egg, slightly beaten
2 tablespoons milk
1 tablespoon butter, softened
1/2 teaspoon cinnamon

Glaze:

1/2 cup powdered sugar

1 tablespoon lemon juice

Filling: Combine sugar, red-hots, cornstarch, water and cherry juice. Cook over medium heat until thickened, stirring occasionally. Stir in cherries. Pour into 8-in., square pan. **Rounds:** Sift flour, baking powder and salt together. Add 3 tablespoons brown sugar and pecans. Cut in shortening to make fine crumbs. Combine egg and milk; add to flour mixture. Mix until all particles are moistened, adding few drops of milk if necessary. Roll out on floured surface to 14- x 12-in. rectangle. Brush with butter. Combine 3 tablespoons brown sugar and cinnamon; sprinkle over dough. Roll up, starting from 12-in. side. Cut into 3/4-in. slices. Place on filling. Bake at 400° for 25 to 30 minutes. **Glaze:** Combine powdered sugar and lemon juice. Spread over cobbler while still warm. **—Judy Olney, Flaxton, North Dakota**

CHERRY-LEMON CREAM CRUNCH

Crust:

1 cup flour, sifted
1/2 teaspoon salt
1/2 teaspoon cinnamon
1/2 cup butter
1/2 cup brown sugar

1 teaspoon vanilla
1 cup shredded coconut
1/2 cup quick, rolled oats
1/2 cup chopped walnuts

Filling:

1/4 cup lemon juice
1 14-ounce can sweetened
condensed milk
4 teaspoons lemon rind, grated

1/2 teaspoon salt
2 eggs
1 21-ounce can cherry pie filling

Crust: Sift together flour, salt and cinnamon. Cream butter; gradually add brown sugar and vanilla. Cream well. Add seasoned flour; stir in coconut, oats and nuts. Press crumb mixture into 13- x 9-in. pan, reserving scant 1/4 cup. Bake at 375° for 12 minutes. **Filling:** Gradually stir lemon juice into sweetened condensed milk until mixture becomes thick. Add lemon rind and salt. Beat eggs slightly; stir slowly into thickened mixture. DO NOT COOK! Spread over baked crust. Top with spoonfuls of cherry pie filling. Sprinkle with remaining crumb mixture. Bake 15 to 18 minutes more. Refrigerate until well chilled. Serve with ice cream or whipped cream if desired. Serves 14. **—Carol Sullivan, Paisley, Oregon**

CHERRY-WALNUT DELIGHT

Crust:

1-1/4 cups flour, sifted
1/2 cup brown sugar
1/2 cup butter

1/2 cup flaked coconut
1/2 cup walnuts, finely chopped

Filling:

1 8-ounce package cream
cheese
1/3 cup sugar
1 egg

1 teaspoon vanilla
1 21-ounce can cherry pie filling
1/2 cup walnuts, coarsely
chopped

Crust: Combine flour, brown sugar and butter. Blend to fine crumbs. Add coconut and finely chopped nuts; mix well. Reserve 1/2 cup of crumb mixture. Press remaining mixture onto bottom of greased, 13- x 9-in. pan. Bake at 350° for 12 to 15 minutes or until edges are very lightly browned. **Filling:** Beat cream cheese until fluffy. Add sugar, egg and vanilla. Spread over hot, baked layer; bake 10 minutes longer. Spread pie filling over cheese layer. Sprinkle with coarsely chopped nuts and reserved crumb mixture. Bake 15 minutes more. Cool; cut into squares.

—Winifred Rushmore, Morley, Michigan

CHERRY COCONUT DESSERT

Crumb Base:

1 cup flour
1/2 teaspoon salt
1-1/4 cups quick oatmeal
3/4 cup brown sugar, firmly
    packed

1/2 cup coconut, flaked or
    shredded
1/2 cup butter, melted

Topping:

1 16-ounce can red, tart, pitted
    cherries, drained
1/2 cup sugar

1/2 teaspoon almond extract
2 tablespoons cornstarch
1/4 cup cold water

Crumb Base: Combine flour, salt, oatmeal, brown sugar, coconut and butter until crumbly. Press half of mixture into lightly greased, 9-in. square pan. **Topping:** Cook cherries, sugar and almond extract together, stirring constantly; when mixture comes to boil, add cornstarch dissolved in water. Continue to cook, stirring, until thick. Spread over crumbs. Sprinkle remaining crumb mixture over top. Bake at 375º for 30 minutes or until golden brown. —**Kathryn Hanks, Carthage, Illinois**

CHERRY-RHUBARB CRUNCH

Crust:

1-1/4 cups oatmeal
1-1/4 cups brown sugar
Pinch salt

1-1/2 cups flour
3/4 cup butter
1/2 cup chopped nuts

Filling:

4 cups diced rhubarb
1 cup sugar
2 tablespoons cornstarch
1 cup water

Few drops almond extract
Few drops red food coloring,
    optional
1 21-ounce can cherry pie filling

Crust: Mix oatmeal, brown sugar, salt, flour and butter with pastry blender until crumbly. Press half of mixture onto bottom of 13- x 9-in. pan. **Filling:** Place rhubarb on top of unbaked crust. Mix sugar, cornstarch and water in saucepan. Cook, stirring, until thick. Add almond extract, food coloring and cherry pie filling. Mix well; spoon over rhubarb. Sprinkle remaining crumb mixture over top; scatter with chopped nuts. Bake about 40 minutes at 350º. Serve plain, with vanilla ice cream or with whipped topping. —**Mrs. Wayne Suhr, Mantorville, Minnesota**

CRUSTS: *When using a graham cracker or cookie crumb crust, it is best to cool the baked shell before filling. (Some recipes call for an unbaked crumb crust.)*

Independence Puffs

CHERRY CREAM PUFFS

Puffs:
1 cup water
1/2 cup butter

1 cup flour, sifted
4 eggs

Filling:
1 21-ounce can cherry pie filling,
   divided

1/2 cup flaked coconut
1 pint whipping cream, whipped

Puffs: Bring water and butter to rolling boil; stir in sifted flour all at once. Stir vigorously over low heat until mixture leaves sides of pan and forms ball, about 1 minute. Remove from heat. Add eggs, one at a time, beating until smooth after each addition. Drop from spoon onto ungreased baking sheet or muffin tin. Heap each mound higher in center; leave about 2 in. between mounds. Bake at 400° for 45 to 50 minutes or until dry. Allow to cool slowly. Cut off tops; spoon out excess dough. **Filling:** Set aside 1/2 cup cherry pie filling. To remaining filling add coconut. Fold in whipped cream. Fill each puff with whipped cream mixture. Replace tops; spoon reserved cherry pie filling over puffs. Serves 8. **—Ruth Pool, Melvin, Illinois**

CHERRY DUMPLINGS

Sauce:
2 tablespoons butter
1/2 cup sugar
1-1/2 cups pitted, red, tart cherries,
   drained, reserving juice

1-1/2 cups boiling water
1/8 teaspoon salt
1/2 cup reserved cherry juice

Dumplings:
1 cup sifted flour
1-1/2 teaspoons baking powder
1/2 teaspoon salt
1/4 cup sugar

2 tablespoons butter
1/2 teaspoon vanilla extract
1/3 to 1/2 cup milk

Sauce: Combine butter, sugar, cherries, water, salt and cherry juice in heavy skillet or large saucepan. Bring to boil. Reduce heat; simmer gently about 5 minutes. **Dumplings:** Sift together flour, baking powder, salt and sugar. Cut in butter until mixture is crumbly. Combine vanilla extract with milk; add to flour mixture, stirring only enough to moisten flour. Drop by spoonfuls into simmering sauce. Cook uncovered for 5 minutes. Cover; steam gently 15 minutes. Serve dumplings warm with cherry sauce. Top with whipped cream, if desired. **—Helen L. Swayne, Gordon, Nebraska**

FEBRUARY DUTCH BABIES

6 eggs
3/4 cup flour
1/2 teaspoon salt
1 cup milk

1/4 cup plus 2 teaspoons melted butter, divided
1 21-ounce can cherry pie filling
1/2 pint whipping cream, whipped

Heat six 10-ounce custard cups in 450° oven until hot. Meanwhile, beat eggs well. Mix flour and salt. Beat into eggs in two additions; mix until smooth. Add half of milk at a time, stirring until well blended after each addition. Add 1/4 cup of butter. Grease insides of custard cups with 2 teaspoons melted butter using pastry brush. Pour 1/2 cup batter into each cup. Bake at 450° for 10 to 15 minutes. As they bake, they will form cups. Prick each center with fork several times. Reduce heat to 350°. Bake 10 minutes longer. Remove to warm platter. Fill with cherry pie filling. Top with whipped cream. Serves 6.   **—Mary Christine Meifeld, Sauk City, Wisconsin**

CHERRY PUFF

1 20-ounce can tart, red, pitted cherries, drained, reserving juice
1/2 cup reserved cherry juice
1/2 cup sugar
2 tablespoons quick tapioca

2 egg whites
1/8 teaspoon salt
1/4 teaspoon cream of tartar
2 egg yolks
1/3 cup sugar
6 tablespoons cake flour, sifted

Crush cherries with potato masher; add cherry liquid, sugar and tapioca. Simmer 5 minutes, stirring constantly. Pour into 1-1/2 quart casserole. Beat egg whites until foamy; add salt and cream of tartar; beat until stiff. Beat yolks until thick and lemon-colored. Add sugar; beat thoroughly. Fold sweetened yolks into egg whites; then fold in flour. Pour over cherry mixture. Bake at 325° for 40 minutes. Serve warm. Serves 6.

—Armida Masterson, Washington, Iowa

SOUR CHERRY FRITTERS

1 cup flour
1 to 2 tablespoons sugar
1/2 teaspoon salt
1 teaspoon baking powder
1 egg
1 tablespoon butter, melted

1/3 cup milk
3/4 cup pitted, tart, red cherries, drained
Cooking oil
Confectioners' sugar

Mix dry ingredients. Beat egg; add melted butter. Combine with milk. Add to dry ingredients. Fold in cherries. Drop by teaspoonfuls into deep, 375° fat. Fry 4 minutes or until browned. Drain on paper. Dust with confectioners' sugar.   **—Debra Frisco, Rochester, Vermont**

Anytime Treats

Traditional Cherry Cakes

CHOCOLATE-CHERRY UPSIDE DOWN CAKE

Topping:

    6 tablespoons butter
    1/4 cup brown sugar

    2 20-ounce cans pitted, dark,
        sweet cherries, drained,
        reserving juice

Cake:

    3 tablespoons butter
    1/2 cup brown sugar
    1/2 cup sugar
    1 egg yolk
    2 squares unsweetened
        chocolate, melted in
        double boiler
    1 cup flour

    1-1/2 teaspoons baking powder
    1/4 teaspoon salt
    1/2 teaspoon cinnamon
    3/4 cup milk
    1 teaspoon vanilla extract
    1 egg white, stiffly beaten
    1/2 pint heavy cream

Topping: Slowly melt butter and sugar in 9-in. iron skillet. Spread evenly over skillet; remove from heat. Place cherries onto butter mixture. **Cake:** Cream butter, brown sugar and granulated sugar until very light. Add egg yolk and melted chocolate; mix thoroughly. Sift together flour, baking powder, salt and cinnamon. Add to chocolate mixture alternately with milk. Add vanilla; mix well. Fold in stiffly beaten egg white. Carefully spoon into skillet so as not to disarrange cherries. Bake at 350º about 45 minutes or until springy to touch. Remove from oven; loosen sides if necessary. Let stand 10 minutes without removing from skillet; invert cake onto serving plate. Let stand 10 minutes more. Lift skillet off slowly. Cool. Whip cream until thick, adding cherry juice by teaspoonfuls until bright pink in color and rich in taste. Spoon onto sides and around edge of top, leaving cherries exposed in center of cake.   **—Debra Frisco, Rochester, Vermont**

DUTCH CHERRY CAKE

    2 cups flour
    2-1/4 teaspoons baking powder
    1/2 teaspoon salt
    1 cup sugar, divided
    2 eggs, separated

    1/2 cup milk
    1/3 cup butter, melted
    1 quart cherries, drained
    1 tablespoon brown sugar
    1 teaspoon cinnamon

Sift flour, baking powder, salt and 3/4 cup sugar together. Beat egg yolks. Add milk and butter; quickly stir into flour mixture until batter is just smooth. Beat egg whites to soft peaks; beat in remaining 1/4 cup sugar until stiff. Fold sugared egg whites and cherries into batter. Pour into greased, 9-in. square baking dish. Sprinkle with brown sugar and cinnamon. Bake at 400º for 35 minutes.   **—Diana L. Bogart, Decatur, Michigan**

CHERRY CARAMEL CAKE

Cake:

1-1/2 cups sugar
3/4 cup shortening
3 eggs
1-1/2 teaspoons baking soda
1-1/2 teaspoons cinnamon

2-1/4 cups flour
3/4 cup sour milk
2 to 2-1/2 cups cherries, fresh, frozen (thawed) or canned

Frosting:

6 tablespoons butter
1/2 cup brown sugar
1/3 cup milk

1-1/2 cups confectioners' sugar
1/2 teaspoon vanilla
1/4 teaspoon salt

Cake: Cream sugar and shortening. Beat in eggs. Sift together baking soda, cinnamon and flour. Fold in dry ingredients and sour milk alternately, beginning and ending with dry ingredients. Fold in cherries. Pour into greased, floured, 13- x 9-in. pan. Bake at 350° for 45 minutes. **Frosting:** Melt butter; add brown sugar and milk. Bring to boil; cook for 2 minutes. Remove from heat. Cool. Beat in confectioners' sugar, vanilla and salt.

—Marilyn Miller, Random Lake, Wisconsin

CHERRY DREAM

1/2 baked angel food cake
1 21-ounce can cherry pie filling
1-1/2 cups milk

1 cup sour cream
1 3-1/2-ounce box instant vanilla pudding mix

Tear cake into small pieces. Arrange half of pieces on bottom of 11- x 8-in. pan. Cover with cherry pie filling. Place remaining cake on top. Combine milk and sour cream; add pudding mix, blending with hand beater. (Don't mix for more than 1 minute to keep from thickening.) Pour quickly over cherry and cake layers; smooth with spatula. Place in refrigerator for about 8 hours before serving. Serve plain or with dollop of whipped cream.

—Vera Emmert Johansen, Ridott, Illinois

SURPRISE CHERRY CAKE

3 eggs
1 cup sugar
2/3 cup vegetable oil
2 tablespoons grated orange rind

2 cups cake flour
1 tablespoon baking powder
1 21-ounce can cherry pie filling
1/4 cup orange juice

Beat eggs and sugar; add oil and orange rind. Mix well. Add flour sifted with baking powder. Pour a little more than half of batter into greased, 11- x 8-in. pan. Cover with cherry pie filling. Add orange juice to remaining batter. Pour over cherry layer, covering cherries completely. Bake 50 minutes at 300°. Serve warm.
—Donna Miller, Towner, North Dakota

CHERRY ANGEL ROLL

1 package angel food cake mix
Confectioners' sugar
3 tablespoons cornstarch
3/4 cup sugar
1/8 teaspoon salt
1 20-ounce can tart, red, pitted cherries, drained, reserving juice

3/4 cup reserved cherry juice
2 tablespoons butter
1/4 teaspoon red food coloring
6 drops almond extract
1/2 pint whipping cream, whipped

Prepare cake according to package directions. Pour batter into well-greased, 15-1/2- x 10-1/2- x 1-in. sheet pan. Bake for 20 minutes at 350⁰. Loosen sides, and turn cake out onto towel sprinkled with confectioners' sugar. Roll cake and towel together; place on rack to cool. Combine cornstarch, sugar and salt. Heat cherry juice in small pan. Gradually stir in sugar mixture. Cook, stirring, until thickened and clear. Add butter, food coloring and almond flavoring. Mash cherries with fork; add to syrup. Unroll cake; trim edges with kitchen shears if necessary. Spread with filling. Roll up; frost with whipped cream. Chill before serving. Serves 10.

—Mrs. Herbert Legler, Eagan, Minnesota

CHERRY-CHIP CAKE

2 cups flour
1 cup sugar
2 teaspoons baking soda
1/4 teaspoon salt
1/2 teaspoon cinnamon
1 21-ounce can cherry pie filling
1 8-1/4-ounce can crushed pineapple

2 eggs, slightly beaten
1/3 cup butter, melted
1 6-ounce package chocolate chips
1/2 cup chopped nuts
1/2 pint whipping cream, whipped

Sift flour, sugar, baking soda, salt and cinnamon together. Stir half of cherry pie filling and all of undrained pineapple into dry ingredients. Blend in eggs. Slowly stir in melted butter. Spread in greased, 13- x 9-in. pan. Sprinkle chips and nuts over top. Bake at 350⁰ for 30 minutes. Serve topped with remaining cherries and whipped cream. **—Judy Garnett, Morley, Michigan**

INSTANT CHERRY CAKE

1 package cake mix, chocolate or white
1 21-ounce can cherry pie filling

2 eggs
2 teaspoons almond flavoring

Combine all ingredients in mixing bowl. Stir only until mixed. Pour into greased, 13- x 9-in. pan; bake at 350⁰ for 30 minutes or until toothpick inserted in center comes out clean. Serve warm with ice cream or cooled topped with whipped cream. **—Nina Nachtigall, Salt Lake City, Utah**

CHERRY CHUCKLE CAKE

Fruit Layer:

6 cups pitted, tart, red cherries, fresh or frozen (thawed and drained)

1-1/2 cups sugar

1 3-ounce package cherry gelatin

4 cups miniature marshmallows

Batter:

2 cups flour

3 teaspoons baking powder

1 cup sugar

1/2 cup shortening

2 eggs

1 teaspoon vanilla

1/2 pint whipping cream, whipped

Fruit layer: Combine cherries, sugar, gelatin and marshmallows; spread in greased, 13- x 9-in. pan. **Batter:** Sift flour and baking powder together. Cream sugar and shortening; add eggs and vanilla. Combine with flour mixture; beat 2 minutes. Pour over fruit layer. Bake at 350° for 30 to 45 minutes or until toothpick inserted in center comes out clean. Cool. Serve with whipped cream. **—Mrs. Norman Moss, Rockland, Idaho**

CHEF'S DELIGHT CHERRY DESSERT

1 angel food cake, baked

1 3-ounce package cherry gelatin

1 cup boiling water

1 21-ounce can cherry pie filling

1 cup whipping cream, whipped

Dissolve gelatin in boiling water. Chill. Meanwhile, cut cake into cubes; line 13- x 9-in. pan with cake. When gelatin is syrupy, fold in cherry pie filling. Spoon over cake. Chill. Cover with layer of whipped cream before serving.
—Corrine Rahman, Plainview, Minnesota

Mt. Vernon Muffins

E.Z. CHERRY PUFFS

1 16-ounce can dark, sweet, cherries, drained

1 egg

1/2 teaspoon vanilla

3 cups buttermilk biscuit mix

1 cup lemon sherbet

1 cup pineapple sherbet

1 teaspoon cinnamon

2 tablespoons sugar

Pit and dice cherries. Lightly beat egg and vanilla. Combine biscuit mix, sherbets and egg. Fold in cherries. Spoon into greased muffin cups, filling each 2/3 full. Combine cinnamon and sugar. Sprinkle over muffins. Bake at 375° for 15 to 20 minutes. Makes 16 muffins.
—Cynthia Kannenberg, Brown Deer, Wisconsin

CHERRY MUFFIN DESSERT

Muffins:

1 egg
1 cup sugar
3 tablespoons butter
1-1/4 cups flour
1 teaspoon baking powder
1/2 teaspoon salt
1/2 cup milk
3/4 cup pitted, tart, red cherries, drained, reserving juice
1/2 cup chopped nuts

Sauce:

2 tablespoons butter
1 tablespoon flour
1 cup cherry juice
1/2 cup sugar

Muffins: Beat egg; blend in sugar and butter. Sift dry ingredients; add to egg mixture. Add milk. Fold in cherries and nuts. Pour into greased muffin pan. Bake at 350º for 30 minutes. **Sauce:** Blend butter and flour. Add cherry juice and sugar. Cook until thickened, stirring constantly. Spoon over warm muffin halves. **—Mary Lou Baryenbruch, Spring Green, Wisconsin**

CHERRY MUFFINS

1 cup frozen or canned cherries, drained
2 cups flour
4 teaspoons baking powder
1 cup sugar, divided
1 teaspoon salt
2 eggs
1/2 cup butter, melted
1 cup milk
1/4 to 1/2 teaspoon cinnamon

Cut cherries into halves. Combine flour, baking powder, 3/4 cup sugar and 1 teaspoon salt in mixing bowl; toss in cherries to coat. In small bowl beat eggs. Add butter and milk; stir into flour mixture just to blend. DO NOT OVERMIX! Fill muffin cups 3/4 full. Sprinkle lightly with mixture of 1/4 cup sugar and cinnamon to taste. Bake at 400º about 15 minutes, until lightly browned. Makes 20 muffins.   **—Nellie E. Schwartz, Milwaukee, Wisconsin**

Homemade Breads

CHERRY CELEBRATION BREAD

Bread:

2/3 cup shortening
1-1/4 cups sugar
3 eggs
4 cups flour
1 teaspoon salt
1 teaspoon baking soda
2 teaspoons baking powder
2 cups applesauce
1 16-ounce can water-packed, pitted, tart, red cherries, drained, reserving juice
1 cup chopped nuts
2 teaspoons almond extract

Glaze:
- 1 cup confectioners' sugar
- 2 tablespoons reserved cherry juice
- 1 tablespoon butter
- 1 teaspoon almond extract

Bread: Cream shortening and sugar. Add eggs. Mix flour, salt, baking soda and baking powder; add to creamed mixture alternately with applesauce. Fold in cherries, nuts and extract. Pour into two greased, 9- x 5-in. loaf pans. Bake 1 to 1-1/4 hours at 350º. Remove from pans while warm. Cool. **Glaze:** Mix together confectioners' sugar, cherry juice, butter and extract until smooth. Spread over cooled loaves. Decorate with maraschino cherries if desired.   **—Kathryn Hanks, Carthage, Illinois**

OATMEAL CHERRY BRAIDS

Bread:
- 1 cup dry oatmeal
- 2 cups hot water
- 1 teaspoon salt
- 3 tablespoons butter
- 2 packages dry yeast
- 1/2 cup very warm water
- 1 tablespoon sugar
- 2/3 cup brown sugar, packed
- 4 to 5 cups flour
- 1 21-ounce can cherry pie filling
- 1-1/2 teaspoons lemon rind, grated

Glaze:
- 1/2 cup confectioners' sugar
- 2 teaspoons hot milk
- 1/4 teaspoon vanilla

Bread: Stir oatmeal into hot water; add salt and butter. Cool to lukewarm. Dissolve yeast in warm water; stir in 1 tablespoon sugar until dissolved. When yeast mixture starts to bubble, add to oatmeal mixture. Stir in brown sugar and enough flour to make stiff dough. Knead until smooth. Cover; let rise until doubled. Punch down dough; divide into three portions. Roll one portion into 10- x 6-in. rectangle. Place on lightly greased baking sheet; spoon 1/3 of cherry pie filling lengthwise down center of dough. Sprinkle with 1/2 teaspoon lemon rind. Cut 10 1-in. strips on each side of filling to with 1/2 in. of filling. (Cut strips almost perpendicular to filling.) Starting with top right strip, overlap dough over filling. Alternate bringing left and right strips over filling, pinching lightly to seal. Let rise until almost doubled. Repeat with remaining dough. Bake at 350º for 20 to 25 minutes. **Glaze:** Combine confectioners' sugar, milk and vanilla. While braids are slightly warm, frost with glaze. **Note:** You may want to make two braids instead of three and use the remaining dough for dinner rolls.

—Carole Burke, Waucoma, Iowa

LEFTOVER PIE FILLING: *If your pie is small, put the leftover filling into small dishes. Top with prepared whipped topping for an extra dessert.*

AFTERNOON TEA BREAD

4 cups baking powder biscuit mix
1/4 cup sugar
1 teaspoon cinnamon
1/4 teaspoon salt
1 16-ounce can tart cherry pie
  filling
1/3 cup milk
1 egg, beaten
1/4 cup butter, melted
1 teaspoon vanilla
1/4 teaspoon almond extract
1 cup chopped, toasted pecans

Combine biscuit mix, sugar, cinnamon and salt. Stir in pie filling, milk, egg, butter, vanilla and almond extract. Mix until blended. Fold in nuts. Pour into two greased, 9- x 5-in. loaf pans. Bake at 350° for 1-1/4 hours. Cool in pans. Serve plain, with butter or spread with whipped cream cheese.

—Cynthia Kannenberg, Brown Deer, Wisconsin

CHERRY ROLLS

Rolls:

1 egg
3/4 cup sour cream
2 cups flour, sifted
1/4 teaspoon baking soda
2-1/2 teaspoons baking powder
3/4 teaspoon salt
2 tablespoons butter, softened
2 cups tart, red, pitted cherries,
  drained, reserving juice
2 tablespoons sugar
1 teaspoon cinnamon

Sauce:

1/3 cup brown sugar
1/3 cup sugar
1-1/2 tablespoons cornstarch
1-1/2 cups reserved cherry juice
1/2 teaspoon almond extract
Few drops red food coloring
1-1/2 tablespoons butter

Rolls: Beat egg and sour cream. Sift together flour, baking soda, baking powder and salt. Add to egg mixture; stir until well mixed. Toss onto lightly floured board; roll out to rectangle 1/4-in. thick. Spread lightly with soft butter; cover with cherries. Sprinkle with combined sugar and cinnamon. Roll up like jelly roll; cut into slices 1-1/4-in. thick. Place slices close together in greased baking pan. **Sauce:** Combine sugars and cornstarch; add cherry juice, almond extract and coloring. Bring to boil. When slightly thickened, add butter; pour over unbaked rolls. Bake at 375° for 25 minutes. Makes 12 rolls.

—Rosa Lohr, Kentland, Indiana

PITTING CHERRIES: *There are several ways to pit cherries. You may want to cut cherries down the center just far enough to remove the pits. A hairpin or pen point inserted in a clean holder also makes an effective cherry pitting utensil.*

Colonial Coffee Cakes

GERMAN CHERRY COFFEE CAKE

Cake:

1 package yeast
1/4 cup warm water
4-1/2 cups flour, divided
1 cup plus 1 tablespoon sugar, divided

1 cup warm milk, divided
1/3 cup butter, melted and cooled
1 teaspoon vanilla

Topping:

1 cup butter, melted
1 cup sugar

1-1/2 cups pitted, tart, red cherries, drained
2 eggs, beaten

Cake: Dissolve yeast in warm water. Place 2-1/2 cups flour in large bowl. Add 1 tablespoon sugar, 2/3 cup warm milk and dissolved yeast, stirring well. Let rise. Add remaining 1 cup sugar, 1/3 cup warm milk, butter and vanilla. Stir well. Add about 2 cups more flour, stirring until blended. Divide dough in half; spread evenly in two 8-in. square, greased pans. Prick dough with fork. Let rise 45 minutes. **Topping:** To melted butter add sugar. Add cherries. Cool mixture. Blend in beaten eggs. Pour over risen dough. Bake at 350° for 40 to 45 minutes.   **—Marcie Wisnieski, Dodge, Nebraska**

CHERRY-FILLED COFFEE CAKE

Cake:

3 cups flour
1 teaspoon baking powder
1 teaspoon baking soda
1 cup sugar
1 cup butter

2 eggs, beaten
1 cup dairy sour cream
1 teaspoon vanilla
1 31-ounce can cherry pie filling

Topping:

1/2 cup sugar
1/2 cup flour

2 tablespoons butter, melted
Whipped cream, optional

Cake: In large mixing bowl combine flour, baking powder, baking soda and sugar. Cut in butter until crumbly. Add beaten eggs, sour cream and vanilla, mixing until creamy. Spread half of batter in greased, 13- x 9- x 2-in. baking pan. Spread cherries evenly over batter, using slotted spoon to drain some of juice. Drop remaining batter by spoonfuls evenly over cherries. Spread batter lightly to cover cherries. (Some filling may show.) **Topping:** Combine sugar, flour and butter, stirring with fork to make crumbs; sprinkle over batter. Bake at 375° for 40 minutes. Serve warm or cold with dollop of whipped cream.   **—Marlene Bomgardner, Annville, Pennsylvania**

CHERRY CRUNCH COFFEE CAKE

Cake:

1-1/2 cups flour
1-1/2 teaspoons baking powder
 1/2 teaspoon salt
 1/4 cup butter

1 cup sugar
2 eggs
1/2 cup milk
1 21-ounce can cherry pie filling

Topping:

 1/2 cup brown sugar
 2 tablespoons flour

2 tablespoons butter

Cake: Sift flour, baking powder and salt together. Cream butter and sugar. Add eggs. Beat well. Blend in milk and dry ingredients. Pour half of batter into 9-in. square, greased baking pan. Cover with cherry pie filling. Pour remaining batter over cherries. **Topping:** Mix brown sugar, flour and butter. Sprinkle over batter. Bake at 350º for 45 minutes.

—**Mary Ellen Hoover, Schwenksville, Pennsylvania**

FRUIT SWIRL COFFEE CAKE

Coffee cake:

1-1/2 cups sugar
 1/2 cup butter
 1/2 cup shortening
1-1/2 teaspoons baking powder
 4 eggs

1 teaspoon vanilla
1 teaspoon almond extract
3 cups flour
1 21-ounce can cherry pie filling

Glaze:

1 cup confectioners' sugar

1 to 2 tablespoons milk

Coffee cake: Blend sugar, butter, shortening, baking powder, eggs, vanilla and almond extract; beat for 3 minutes on high speed. Stir in 3 cups flour. Spread 2/3 of batter in bottom of greased jelly roll pan or two 9-in. square pans. Spoon pie filling over batter. Drop remaining batter by tablespoonfuls onto pie filling. Bake at 350º for 45 minutes. **Glaze:** Mix together confectioners' sugar and milk. Drizzle over warm coffee cake.

—**Linda Morgan, Kidder, Missouri**

CHOCOLATE CHERRY CAKE

 2 cups flour
3/4 cup sugar
3/4 cup oil
 2 eggs
 2 teaspoons vanilla
 1 teaspoon baking soda
 1 teaspoon cinnamon

1/8 teaspoon salt
 1 21-ounce can cherry pie filling
 1 6-ounce package semi-sweet
 chocolate morsels
 1 cup chopped nuts
Confectioners' sugar

Combine flour, sugar, oil, eggs, vanilla, baking soda, cinnamon and salt. Mix well. Stir in cherry pie filling, chocolate morsels and nuts. Pour into greased, floured, 9-cup bundt pan or 10-in. tube pan. Bake at 350° for 1 hour. Cool 10 minutes; remove from pan. Cool completely. Sprinkle top with confectioners' sugar. —**Sharon Thornsbrough, Williamsport, Indiana**

CHERRY CRUMB COFFEE CAKE

2 cups plus 3 tablespoons flour
1-1/2 cups sugar
3/4 cup butter
2 eggs, separated
1 teaspoon salt

1 teaspoon vanilla
1/2 teaspoon almond extract
2 teaspoons baking powder
1 cup milk
1 21-ounce can cherry pie filling

Blend flour, sugar and butter until crumbs resemble coarse meal. Set aside 1 cup for topping. Add egg yolks, salt, vanilla, almond extract, baking powder and milk. Mix until smooth. Beat egg whites until stiff; fold into flour mixture. Pour into greased, lightly floured, 13- x 9-in. pan or two 8-in. pie pans. Spoon cherry pie filling over top of batter. Sprinkle reserved crumbs over top of fruit. Bake at 350° for 30 to 40 minutes. Drizzle warm cake with thin, powdered sugar icing flavored with almond extract.

—**Mrs. Delbert Heuer, Fountain City, Wisconsin**

COLONIAL COFFEE CAKE

2 cups flour, divided
1 teaspoon double-acting baking
  powder
1/4 teaspoon baking soda
1/4 teaspoon salt
1 cup sugar, divided
1/2 cup milk

1 egg
1 teaspoon vanilla extract
1/2 cup plus 3 tablespoons melted
  butter, divided
1/4 teaspoon lemon extract
1 21-ounce can cherry pie filling

With fork mix 1-1/4 cups flour, baking powder, baking soda, salt and 1/2 cup sugar in a large bowl. Add milk, egg, vanilla extract and 1/2 cup butter; beat with spoon until well blended. Pour into greased and floured, 9-in. square pan. Combine remaining 3/4 cup flour, 1/2 cup sugar and 3 tablespoons butter, mixing with fork to form coarse crumbs. Sprinkle half of crumb mixture on top of batter. Stir lemon extract into cherry pie filling; spread over batter. Sprinkle with remaining crumb mixture. Bake 1 hour or until golden in 350° oven. Cool slightly. Cut into squares; serve warm. **Note:** Drizzle powdered sugar icing over warm cake if desired.

—**Judi Nuest, Kouts, Indiana**

CHERRY-GO-ROUND

Dough:

1 package dry yeast
1/4 cup warm water
1 cup milk, scalded
1/2 cup sugar

1 teaspoon salt
1/2 cup butter
1 egg
4 cups flour, divided

Filling:

1/2 cup brown sugar
1/2 cup flour
1/2 cup pecans

1-1/2 cups tart, pitted, red cherries, well drained

Frosting:

1 cup confectioners' sugar, sifted

1 tablespoon milk
1/2 teaspoon vanilla

Dough: Dissolve yeast in warm water. To scalded milk add sugar, salt and butter; cool to lukewarm. Combine with yeast. Add egg and 2 cups flour. Beat until smooth. Stir in remaining flour to make stiff dough. Cover tightly. Refrigerate between 2 hours and 2 days, or let rise at room temperature until doubled in bulk. Roll dough into two 14- x 7-in. rectangles. **Filling:** Combine brown sugar, flour and pecans. Spread cherries on dough; sprinkle with brown sugar mixture. Roll up each rectangle lengthwise; seal edges. Form into 2 rings. Place sealed edges down on greased baking sheets. Seal ends. Cut slits 2/3 through rolls at 1-in. intervals. Twist each section slightly. Cover; let rise in warm place for 1 hour or until doubled in bulk. Bake at 375° for 25 minutes. **Frosting:** Blend powdered sugar, milk and vanilla together. Drizzle over warm pastry. **Note:** Cherry-Go-Round may be frozen after baking and frosted when thawed. **—Janice Schleusener, Tomah, Wisconsin**

CHERRY-BANANA BREAKFAST CAKE

1/2 cup butter, softened
1 cup sugar
2 eggs
2 cups flour
1/2 teaspoon baking powder
1/2 teaspoon salt
2 bananas, mashed

1/4 cup orange juice
1/8 cup frosted cornflakes
1/8 cup oatmeal
1/2 cup milk
1/8 cup honey
1 cup tart, red, pitted cherries
1/2 cup chopped nuts

Cream butter and sugar until light and fluffy. Add eggs; beat well. Sift flour with baking powder and salt. Combine bananas, orange juice, cornflakes, oatmeal, milk, honey, cherries and nuts. Add dry ingredients to butter mixture. Blend well. Add fruit mixture. Beat until smooth. Bake in greased, floured bundt pan at 350° for 50 minutes. Cool. Drizzle cooled cake with powdered sugar icing. Garnish with cherries and chopped nuts if desired. Serves 16. **—Cynthia Kannenberg, Brown Deer, Wisconsin**

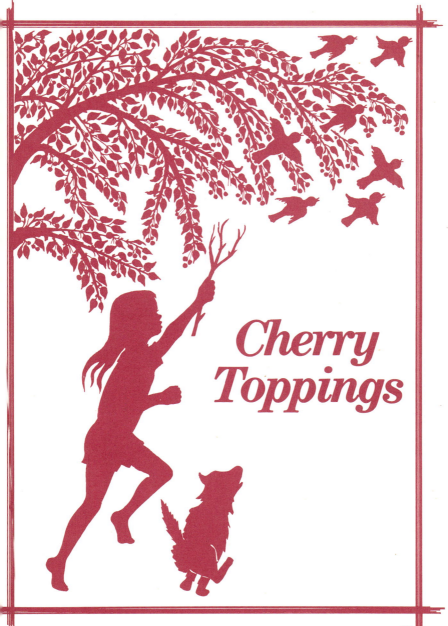

Cherry Toppings

Statemen's Syrups

CHERRY CREPES SUPREME

Batter:

4 eggs
1/2 cup water
1/2 cup milk
1/2 teaspoon salt

2 tablespoons butter, melted
2 teaspoons sugar
1 teaspoon vanilla
1 cup flour

Filling:

8 ounces cream cheese, softened
1/2 cup sugar

1 medium-sized carton frozen whipped topping, thawed

Topping:

3/4 cup water
1 cup sugar
3 tablespoons cornstarch

1 teaspoon vanilla
Few drops red food coloring
1-1/2 cups dark, sweet cherries

Batter: Combine all ingredients except flour. Beat with electric mixer, gradually adding flour. Beat until smooth. Bake on crepe maker. **Filling:** Beat cream cheese and sugar until smooth. Add whipped topping; stir well. **Topping:** Cook water, sugar and cornstarch over medium heat until clear and thick. Stir in vanilla and food coloring. Cool; add cherries. Fill crepes with cream cheese mixture. Roll up jelly roll fashion. Cover each crepe with 2 to 3 tablespoons cherry topping. Serve at room temperature. Yields 12 to 14 crepes. **Note:** Crepes may be prepared and filled ahead of time. Cover with cherry topping at serving time. —**Juanita Jameson, Garden City, Kansas**

CINNAMON WAFFLES WITH CHERRIES

Waffles:

1-3/4 cups all-purpose flour, sifted
3 teaspoons baking powder
2 tablespoons sugar
1 teaspoon cinnamon
1/2 teaspoon salt

1-3/4 cups milk
2 egg yolks
1/4 cup butter, melted
2 egg whites

Topping:

1 21-ounce can cherry pie filling   Whipped cream or ice cream

Waffles: Sift together dry ingredients. Beat milk, egg yolks and butter. Stir into dry ingredients. Beat egg whites to soft peaks; fold into batter. Bake in waffle iron. Makes eight 4-1/2-in. square waffles. **Topping:** Heat cherry pie filling in top of double boiler; serve over waffles. Top with whipped cream or ice cream. —**Elizabeth Netsch, Tomah, Wisconsin**

CHERRY SYRUP

1 tablespoon cornstarch
1/4 cup plus 1 tablespoon water, divided
2 cups pitted cherries, fresh or frozen (thawed)

3/4 cup sugar
1/2 teaspoon almond extract
1/2 teaspoon cinnamon

Mix cornstarch and 1 tablespoon water. Combine cherries, sugar and 1/4 cup water in saucepan. Bring to boil over medium heat, stirring constantly. Gradually stir in dissolved cornstarch. Continue to cook, stirring, until syrup becomes thickened and clear. Stir in almond extract and cinnamon. Serve over pancakes, french toast, waffles or ice cream. Makes 1-1/2 cups.

—Mrs. Benny Muczynski, Youngsville, Pennsylvania

EASY CHERRY OMELET

Omelet:
6 eggs
1/3 cup milk
1/2 teaspoon salt

1/8 teaspoon pepper
1 tablespoon butter

Topping:
1 21-ounce can cherry pie filling

1/4 teaspoon lemon juice

Omelet: Beat eggs slightly; add milk, salt and pepper. Melt butter in omelet pan or skillet; pour in egg mixture. Cook slowly, lifting to let uncooked portion flow underneath. **Topping:** Warm pie filling slowly. Stir in lemon juice. Fold cooked omelet in half. Spoon warm topping over omelet. Serves 4.

—Inez Lenstrom, Rockford, Illinois

CHERRY SUNDAE SAUCE

1/3 cup sugar
2 tablespoons cornstarch
1 cup frozen cherries, thawed, drained, reserving juice

1 cup reserved cherry juice
2 tablespoons lemon juice
Dash cinnamon

Mix sugar and cornstarch in saucepan. Gradually stir in cherry liquid to make smooth mixture. Cook over low to moderate heat, stirring constantly, until sauce is thickened and clear. Add cherries, lemon juice and cinnamon. Cook, stirring, 5 minutes longer. Spoon warm sauce over vanilla ice cream. Serve immediately.

—Wilma Billings, Friendship, Wisconsin

WHIPPING CREAM: *You can whip your cream before guests arrive if you add a little honey or powdered sugar.*

Canning Jar Jams

CHERRY JAM

3 pounds tart, red cherries, fresh
5 cups sugar

1 1-3/4-ounce box powdered fruit
pectin
2 tablespoons lemon juice

Pit and thoroughly grind cherries. Drain. Pack fruit solidly into 4-cup measure, which should be filled. (Use more cherries if necessary.) Measure sugar, and set aside. Stir pectin into prepared fruit in saucepan. Be sure pan is no more than 1/3 full to allow enough room for boiling. Bring to boil over high heat. Immediately stir in sugar all at once. Bring to full, rolling boil; then boil 1 minute. Quickly stir in lemon juice. Immediately pour into sterilized jars. Seal with layer of paraffin. Yields 3 pints.

—Mrs. L.D. Singleton, Exeter, Nebraska

SWISS STYLE CHERRY-CURRANT JAM

6 cups red currants
16 cups bing cherries (4 pounds)

7-1/2 cups sugar

Place stemmed currants in heavy kettle with just enough cold water to cover. Heat slowly; cook until currants are soft. Press through fine sieve or jelly bag. Pit cherries; tie pits in cheesecloth. Return currant juice to kettle, add sugar. Cook, stirring often, until sugar dissolves. Add cherries and bag with pits. Cook slowly until syrupy, about 20 minutes. Remove pits. Pour jam into hot, sterilized glasses; seal.   **—Helen G. West, Davenport, California**

CHERRY-STRAWBERRY JAM

1 pound, ripe, tart, red cherries
1 quart ripe strawberries
4-1/2 cups sugar

1 1-3/4-ounce box powdered
fruit pectin

Pit and finely chop cherries. Thoroughly crush strawberries. Combine fruits Place in saucepan. Pre-measure sugar; set aside. Add powdered fruit pectin to fruit; mix well. Cook over high heat, stirring constantly until mixture comes to hard boil. Immediately stir in sugar. Bring to full, rolling boil; boil hard for 1 minute, stirring constantly. Remove from heat; skim off foam with metal spoon. Stir and skim for 5 minutes to cool slightly and prevent floating fruit. Quickly ladle into sterilized glasses. Cover at once with 1/8-in. hot paraffin. Makes 8 medium-sized glasses of jam.

—Karen Schmidt, Racine, Wisconsin

CHERRY-PEACH JAM

1-1/2 cups tart, pitted and
    chopped, red cherries, fresh,
    frozen or canned
1-1/2 cups pitted, chopped
    peaches, fresh, frozen or canned

1 1-3/4-ounce box powdered
    fruit pectin
4 cups sugar

If using frozen or canned fruits, drain before chopping. Combine cherries and peaches in large saucepan. Add pectin; stir well. Measure sugar; set aside. Bring fruit to rolling boil over high heat. Continue to boil while stirring in sugar. Boil vigorously for 1 minute more. Remove from heat. Pour into hot, sterilized jars; seal. **—Gretchen Weaver, Goshen, Indiana**

SWEET CHERRY AND PINEAPPLE CONSERVE

4 cups pitted, sweet cherries,
    fresh
1 13-1/4-ounce can crushed
    pineapple, drained

4 cups sugar
1/4 cup lemon juice
1/3 cup chopped pecans

Combine cherries, pineapple and sugar. Let stand 1 hour. Bring to boil, stirring several times. Cook hard for 30 to 35 minutes, stirring occasionally. Add lemon juice and pecans. Cook 5 minutes. Pour into hot, sterilized jars. Seal. Makes 5 pints. **—Cynthia Kannenberg, Brown Deer, Wisconsin**

BLACK CHERRY CONSERVE

2 oranges, seeded
1 quart dark, pitted, sweet
    cherries

6 tablespoons lemon juice
3-1/2 cups sugar
3/4 teaspoon cinnamon

Cut oranges into very thin slices. Barely cover with water; cook until very tender. Add cherries, lemon juice, sugar and cinnamon. Simmer until thickened and clear. Pour into jelly glasses. Let conserve cool to point of setting; seal with layer of paraffin.

—Marilyn Rawls, Pomaria, South Carolina

CHERRY-RHUBARB JAM

6 cups rhubarb, finely cut
4 cups sugar

1 21-ounce can cherry pie filling
1 3-ounce package cherry gelatin

Mix rhubarb and sugar; let stand for 12 hours. Bring rhubarb and sugar to boil; simmer for 10 minutes. Add cherry pie filling and cherry gelatin. Cook 1 minute. Pour into sterilized jars; seal immediately.

—Wilma Wolner, St. James, Minnesota

Betsy Ross Relishes

DUCK WITH CHERRY-BRANDY SAUCE

Duck:

1 4-pound duckling, quartered
Salt and freshly ground pepper to taste

1 clove garlic, pressed
1 cup orange juice

Sauce:

1 tablespoon cornstarch
2 tablespoons water
1 16-ounce can pitted, dark, sweet cherries, drained, reserving juice
1-1/2 cups reserved cherry juice
2 teaspoons beef extract

1/4 cup wine vinegar
1/4 cup orange juice
1/4 cup lemon juice
1/4 cup brandy
1/4 cup currant jelly
1 teaspoon orange peel, grated
1 teaspoon lemon peel, grated

Duck: Season poultry with salt and pepper; rub with garlic. Place on rack, skin side up, over deep pan to catch drippings. Roast at 425° for 30 minutes; turn heat down to 350°. Roast 1-1/2 to 2 hours or until tender. Baste several times with orange juice. **Sauce:** Make paste of cornstarch and water. Pour cherry liquid into saucepan. Add beef extract, vinegar, orange and lemon juices, brandy, currant jelly and grated orange and lemon peels. Cook, stirring, for 10 minutes. Stir in cornstarch paste. Continue to cook and stir until clear and slightly thickened. Add cherries. Heat, but do not boil. Makes 3-1/2 cups sauce.   **—Carol Dinkledine, Potosi, Wisconsin**

CHERRY-ALMOND CHICKEN

1 20-ounce can pitted bing cherries, drained
1 8-ounce can white grapes, drained
1 cup diced peaches, fresh or canned (drained)
1/3 cup slivered blanched almonds
3 tablespoons cornstarch

2 cups chicken broth
1/2 teaspoon salt
1/4 to 1/2 teaspoon celery salt
1-1/2 tablespoons lemon juice
2 cups chicken breast, cooked, diced
Cinnamon
Hot fluffy rice

Combine drained fruits and nuts. In 4-quart saucepan combine cornstarch, broth, salt and celery salt to taste. Stir until smooth. Cook over medium heat, stirring constantly, until thickened. Add lemon juice. Stir in fruits and chicken. Reduce heat to low; simmer 5 minutes. Serve hot over cinnamon-dusted rice. Serves 6.   **—Mabel Mantel, Orange City, Iowa**

CHERRY-CROWNED DINNER LOAF

Meat:

1-1/2 cups Italian-seasoned bread
  crumbs
1/2 cup milk
1 pound ground ham
1 pound ground pork
1 tablespoon chopped onion

1 tablespoon chopped shallot
1/3 cup snipped parsley
1/2 teaspoon dry mustard
  powder
2 eggs, beaten

Sauce:

1 16-ounce can tart, red, pitted
  cherries, drained, reserving
  juice
1 cup reserved cherry juice
4 teaspoons cornstarch

2 tablespoons sugar
1/4 teaspoon seasoned salt
1/8 teaspoon cinnamon
1/8 teaspoon allspice
Red food coloring

Meat: Mix bread crumbs and milk. Add ham, pork, onion, shallot, parsley, mustard and eggs. Mix well. Pack into 1-1/2 quart, round baking dish. Bake at 350° for 1 hour. **Sauce:** Stir together cherry liquid, cornstarch, sugar, seasoned salt, cinnamon and allspice. Cook over medium heat, stirring, until thickened and clear. Add cherries and coloring to desired tint. Heat. Remove drippings from meat pan. Unmold loaf onto platter. Spoon cherry sauce over meat. Pass remaining sauce separately. Serves 6.

—Cynthia Kannenberg, Brown Deer, Wisconsin

CHERRY-HAM LOGS

Meat:

1/2 pound ground pork
1 pound ham, coarsely ground
1/2 cup dry bread crumbs
2 eggs, well beaten
1/8 teaspoon ground pepper

1/8 teaspoon ground cloves
12 whole cloves
1/4 cup brown sugar
1 tablespoon prepared mustard
1 tablespoon cider vinegar

Sauce:

1 tablespoon cornstarch
1/4 cup sugar

1 cup pitted, tart, red cherries,
  drained, reserving juice
1 cup reserved cherry juice

Meat: Combine first 6 ingredients, mixing well. Shape into 6 logs. Place in greased pan large enough to leave a little space between logs. Stick 2 cloves into each log. Combine brown sugar, mustard and vinegar; spread over meat. Bake uncovered at 350° for 45 minutes. **Sauce:** Combine cornstarch, sugar and cherry juice. Cook over low heat, stirring, until thickened and clear. Add cherries. Spoon over ham logs. Serves 6.

—Mildred Martin, Cambridge, Wisconsin

CHERRY-ORANGE CHOPS

6 pork loin chops, 1/2-in. thick
1/2 teaspoon salt
1 medium onion, cut into 6 slices
1 6-ounce can frozen orange juice
concentrate, thawed
1/4 cup brown sugar, packed
1/2 teaspoon ground allspice
1/4 cup vinegar
3/4 cup water
1 21-ounce can cherry pie filling
6 thin orange slices

Trim excess fat from chops. Brown in lightly greased skillet. Season chops with salt. Top each chop with onion slice. Mix orange juice concentrate, sugar, allspice, vinegar and water; pour over chops. Heat to boiling. Reduce heat; cover. Simmer 25 to 30 minutes or until tender. Pour cherry pie filling over chops. Arrange orange slices over cherries. Simmer covered until sauce is bubbly, about 15 minutes. Serve over hot rice.

—Gloria Kratz, Des Moines, Iowa

CRANBERRY-CHERRY RELISH

1-1/2 cups cranberries, fresh or
frozen (thawed)
1 orange
1 lemon
2 cups dark brown sugar,
packed
1-1/2 cups raisins
1 cup cherries, fresh, frozen
(thawed) or canned
1/2 cup vinegar
1/2 teaspoon ground cinnamon
1/2 teaspoon ground cloves
1/2 teaspoon ground nutmeg
1/2 stick cinnamon

Rinse cranberries; discard soft berries and stems. Quarter orange and lemon; remove seeds. Cut into small pieces. Combine all ingredients in large saucepan. Mix thoroughly. Bring to boil. Reduce heat; cook 15 minutes more. Remove cinnamon stick. Cool. Relish keeps 2 to 3 weeks in refrigerator, or it may be frozen. Makes 6 cups.

—Jean Hansen, Atlantic, Iowa

HAM SLICES WITH SPICY CHERRY SAUCE

2 tablespoons cornstarch
3/4 cup orange juice
3/4 cup sugar
1 tablespoon lemon juice
1 1-in. stick cinnamon
Dash salt
1 16-ounce can pitted, tart, red
cherries
1/2 teaspoon cloves
Cooked ham slices

Blend together cornstarch and orange juice. Add remaining ingredients except ham. Cook until thickened and clear. Serve warm over cooked ham slices.

—Savilla Mesker, Henderson, Minnesota

MEATBALLS IN CHERRY SAUCE

Cherry Sauce:

1 16-ounce can dark, sweet, pitted cherries, drained, reserving juice

1/4 cup orange juice

2 tablespoons soy sauce

1/4 teaspoon Worcestershire Sauce

1/4 teaspoon orange rind, grated

3 tablespoons vinegar

1 tablespoon cornstarch

3 tablespoons brown sugar

3 tablespoons lemon juice

Meatballs:

1 pound lean ground beef or pork

1/2 cup soft bread crumbs

1 egg

2 tablespoons minced onion

1/4 cup water chestnuts, finely chopped

2 tablespoons milk

3/4 teaspoon salt

1/8 teaspoon pepper

1/4 teaspoon garlic salt

1 teaspoon Worcestershire Sauce

Sauce: Pour cherry syrup into large saucepan. Add remaining sauce ingredients except cherries. Mix well. Cut some cherries into halves and some into quarters. Add to sauce. Cook, stirring, until clear and slightly thickened. Set aside. **Meatballs:** Mix all ingredients well. Shape into 36 balls. Brown slowly in ungreased skillet. Drain well. Add to sauce. Simmer gently 10 to 15 minutes. Serve hot with cocktail picks. **—Carole Burke, Waucoma, Iowa**

LEG OF LAMB WITH SPICY CHERRY SAUCE

Lamb:

3/4 of leg of lamb, with bone

Seasoned salt to taste

Pepper to taste

Sauce:

4 teaspoons cornstarch

1/4 teaspoon cloves

1/4 teaspoon mace

1/4 cup orange juice

1/4 cup water

1 16-ounce can dark, sweet, pitted cherries, drained, reserving juice

1/2 cup reserved cherry juice

1 lemon, sliced

Lamb: Start skewer through butt end of leg, below bone. Push skewer through so that it comes out along top side of shank bone. Test for balance. Season to taste. Place skewer in rotisserie; start motor. Cook to 160 degrees, which will take about 2 hours. **Sauce:** Mix cornstarch with spices in saucepan. Blend in orange juice, water and cherry juice. Add lemon slices. Cook, stirring, until thick and clear. Brush lamb with sauce several times during last 30 minutes of cooking time. Add cherries to sauce just before serving. Pass cherry sauce separately to spoon over. Serves 6. **Note:** If fresh cherries replace canned, use more orange juice and water as substitute for 1/2 cup cherry juice. **—Cynthia Kannenberg, Brown Deer, Wisconsin**

CHERRY GLAZED HAM CUBES

Meat:

2/3 pound ground ham
1-1/3 pounds ground pork
1 cup dry bread crumbs

1/4 teaspoon pepper
2 eggs, beaten
1 cup milk

Glaze:

1 21-ounce can cherry pie filling
1/2 cup golden raisins

2 tablespoons lemon juice
1/4 teaspoon cinnamon

Meat: Combine meats, crumbs, pepper, eggs and milk. Mix thoroughly. Pat into 9-in. square pan. Bake at 350° for 45 minutes. **Glaze:** Combine cherry pie filling and raisins. Stir in lemon juice and cinnamon. Coat meat mixture with cherry glaze. Bake 15 minutes more. When slightly cooled, cut into cubes. **—Ardell Kaufman, Freeman, South Dakota**

CHERRY RELISH

2 cups cherries, pitted
1 cup seedless raisins
1 teaspoon ground cinnamon
1/4 teaspoon ground cloves

1/2 cup honey
1/2 cup vinegar
1 cup broken pecan nut meats

Combine all ingredients except nuts. Cook slowly for 1 hour. Add nuts. Cook 3 minutes longer. Pour into hot, sterilized jars, leaving 1/4-in. headspace. Adjust seals. Process in boiling water bath for 10 minutes. **—Barbara A. Horn, Chase, Kansas**

PICKLED CHERRIES

2-1/2 cups light brown sugar, firmly
      packed
  2 cups cider vinegar
  2 teaspoons whole cloves

4 3-in. cinnamon sticks, broken
2 quarts pitted, tart, red
  cherries

Sterilize 3 pint jars; leave in hot water until ready to fill. Combine sugar, vinegar and spices in large saucepan. Bring to boil. Reduce heat; simmer 3 to 4 minutes. Strain through cheesecloth to remove spices. Cook strained liquid with cherries about 5 minutes or until heated through. Remove from heat; ladle into hot, sterilized jars. Cover with hot liquid. Cap immediately as directed by canning jar manufacturer. **—Lyn Freie, Middletown, Missouri**

CHERRY JUICE: *In recipes calling for juice reserved from draining cherries, add water if necessary to get the full amount of juice.*

*Pretty
as a
Blossom*

Grandma's Cherry Molds

SWEETHEARTS CHERRY DREAM

Mold:

2 tablespoons unflavored gelatin
1 13-1/2-ounce can crushed
 pineapple, drained, reserving
 juice
1/2 cup reserved pineapple juice
1 30-ounce can pitted, dark,
 sweet cherries in heavy syrup,
 drained, reserving syrup

2 cups cottage cheese
1/2 cup sour cream
1/2 cup chopped pecans
1 tablespoon sugar
1 teaspoon lemon rind, grated
1 tablespoon lemon juice
1/8 teaspoon salt
1/2 cup whipping cream, whipped

Sauce:

1/2 cup sugar
2 tablespoons cornstarch
1/8 teaspoon salt
1 cup reserved cherry syrup
1 teaspoon lemon rind, grated

2 tablespoons lemon juice
1 tablespoon reserved pineapple
 juice
1/2 cup reserved cherries

Mold: Soften gelatin in pineapple juice. Cook over low heat, stirring constantly, until gelatin dissolves. Cool slightly. Halve cherries, setting 1/2 cup aside for sauce. Combine remaining cherries, all the pineapple, cottage cheese, sour cream, pecans, sugar, lemon rind, lemon juice, and salt. Add dissolved gelatin. Fold in whipped cream. Pour into 7-cup mold. Chill. **Sauce:** Combine sugar, cornstarch and salt; stir in cherry syrup. Cook over medium heat until thickened, about 2 minutes. Stir in lemon rind and juice, pineapple juice and reserved cherries. Cool. Unmold gelatin mixture onto serving platter. Spoon sauce around outer edge. Pour remaining sauce into bowl to pass separately. Serves 12.

—Cynthia Kannenberg, Brown Deer, Wisconsin

CHERRY VELVET CREAM DESSERT

2 envelopes unflavored gelatin
2 cups milk
1/8 teaspoon salt
3/4 cup sugar

3 eggs, separated
1 pint sour cream
2 teaspoons vanilla
1 21-ounce can cherry pie filling

Combine gelatin, milk, salt and sugar. Cook over medium heat, stirring until gelatin dissolves. Beat egg yolks lightly. Blend gelatin mixture into yolks. Cool. Stir in sour cream and vanilla. Whip egg whites until stiff peaks form. Fold into gelatin mixture. Pour into 7-cup mold. Chill until firm. Unmold onto serving plate. Top with cherry pie filling. Serves 8.

—Teresa Egoian, Tulare, California

CHERRY SALAD

1 3-ounce package cherry
  gelatin
1-1/2 cups hot water

1 cup cherry conserve (recipe
  below)
1 cup diced apples
1/2 cup chopped celery

Dissolve gelatin in hot water; chill until syrupy. Fold in remaining ingredients; spoon into 8 individual molds or ring mold; chill until firm.

—Joyce Garske, New London, Wisconsin

FROZEN CHERRY CONSERVE

5 quarts pitted, tart, red cherries,
  fresh
2 16-ounce cans crushed
  pineapple, drained, reserving
  juice
8 cups sugar

8 teaspoons ascorbic acid
  powder
2 teaspoons cinnamon
1/8 teaspoon ground cloves
2 1-3/4-ounce boxes powdered
  fruit pectin

Chop cherries. (Cherries and juice should measure 12 cups.) Drain cherries, reserving juice. Stir fruits together. Combine sugar, ascorbic acid powder and spices; add to fruit. Mix well; let stand to dissolve sugar. Combine pectin and fruit juices in large kettle. Heat to full, rolling boil; boil 1 minute, stirring constantly. Remove from heat. Add fruit mixture; stir 2 minutes. Ladle into freezer containers; let stand at room temperature about 8 hours, until mixture is jelled. Freeze. Yields 10 pints.

—Joyce Garske, New London, Wisconsin

TART CHERRY SALAD MOLD

1 16-ounce can pitted, tart, red
  cherries, drained, reserving
  juice
1 15-ounce can crushed
  pineapple, drained, reserving
  juice

1-1/2 cups reserved fruit juices
1/2 cup sugar
1 6-ounce package cherry
  gelatin
1-1/4 cups ginger ale
1/2 cup chopped walnuts

To combined cherry and pineapple juices, add sugar. Bring to boil. Stir in gelatin until dissolved. Add cherries, pineapple and ginger ale. Chill until thick but not set. Stir in nuts. Pour into 13- x 9-in. pan. Chill until set. Serves 12 to 15.

—Barbara Kaup, Bassett, Nebraska

CHERRY CONSERVES: *When canning cherry jams or relishes, remember to use a saucepan large enough to allow for boiling the fruit. The saucepan should be no more than 1/3 full.*

JUBILEE SALAD MOLD

1/2 cup currant jelly
2 cups water, divided
1 6-ounce package raspberry
  gelatin
1/4 cup lemon juice

1 10-ounce package frozen
  raspberries, thawed and
  drained, reserving juice
1 16-ounce can pitted, dark,
  sweet cherries, drained

Combine jelly and 1/2 cup water in saucepan. Heat until jelly is melted. Ad[d]
remaining water and gelatin. Heat and stir until gelatin dissolves. Remov[e]
from heat; stir in lemon juice and reserved raspberry juice. Chill until partia[l]
ly set. Fold in cherries and raspberries. Pour into 1-1/2-quart mold. Chill un[til]
til set. Serves 8 to 10.   **—Lorinda Balsiger, Germantown, Wisconsi[n]**

STUFFED CHERRY SALAD MOLD

1 3-ounce package cream cheese,
  softened
1/2 cup chopped nuts
1 cup pitted bing cherries,
  drained, reserving juice

1 3-ounce package lemon gelati[n]
1 cup reserved cherry juice
1 grapefruit, peeled and
  sectioned
1 cup grapefruit juice

Blend cream cheese and nuts. Stuff cherries with mixture. Dissolve gelatin i[n]
hot cherry juice. Add grapefruit juice. Arrange cherries and grapefruit se[c]
tions in bottom of 1-quart mold; add enough gelatin just to cover. Chill unt[il]
firm. Chill remaining gelatin until syrupy. Pour into mold. Chill until firm. Un[-]
mold onto lettuce. Serve with sweetened mayonnaise if desired. Serves [6]
          —Gladys Duha, New Lenox, Illino[is]

CHERRY-CRANBERRY SALAD

2 cups boiling water
1 6-ounce package lemon
  gelatin
1 8-ounce can jellied cranberry
  sauce
1 17-ounce can dark, sweet,
  pitted cherries, drained, reserving juice

1-1/2 cups reserved cherry liquid
1 cup dairy sour cream
1 apple, diced
1/2 cup chopped walnuts

Pour boiling water over gelatin in bowl. Stir until dissolved. Set aside 1/[2]
cup gelatin to cool. Pour remaining gelatin into 1-1/2-quart saucepan. He[at]
with cranberry sauce until sauce is melted. Add cherry juice to cranber[ry]
mixture. Chill until partially set. Combine 1/2 cup reserved lemon gelat[in]
with sour cream. Chill until partially set. Stir halved cherries, apple and nu[ts]
into cranberry mixture. Pour 1/4 cup of mixture into 7-cup mold. Add r[e]
maining cranberry mixture alternately with combined sour cream an[d]
lemon gelatin. Swirl gently with spatula. Chill until firm. Serves 8 to 10.
          —Nina Nachtigall, Salt Lake City, Uta[h]

CHERRY-SPICE MOLD WITH CREAMY DRESSING

Salad:

2 cups pitted, sweet cherries, fresh
1 stick cinnamon
1/2 teaspoon whole cloves
2 cups water

1 6-ounce package cherry gelatin
1 tablespoon lemon juice
1-1/2 cups cold water
1/2 cup chopped pecans

Dressing:

1/2 cup salad dressing
1/2 cup dairy sour cream
1 tablespoon orange juice

1 teaspoon orange peel, grated
2 teaspoons sugar

Salad: Cut cherries in half. Put cinnamon and cloves in saucepan with 2 cups water. Simmer 10 minutes. Remove from heat; set aside for 10 minutes. Strain out spices; pour hot water over gelatin in a bowl. Stir well. Add lemon juice and cold water. Chill until partially set. Stir in cherries and nuts. Pour into 1-quart mold. Chill. **Dressing:** Blend salad dressing and sour cream until smooth. Add orange juice, peel and sugar. Blend well. Unmold salad; spoon dressing over top. Serves 8.

—Cynthia Kannenberg, Brown Deer, Wisconsin

CHERRY-CIDER SALAD

2 cups apple cider or apple juice
1 6-ounce package cherry gelatin
1 16-ounce can pitted, dark, sweet cherries, drained, reserving juice

1-1/2 cups reserved cherry juice
1/2 cup thinly sliced celery
1/2 cup chopped walnuts
1 3-ounce package cream cheese, softened
1 cup applesauce

Bring apple cider or juice to boil. Dissolve gelatin in boiling liquid. Halve cherries, set aside. Stir cherry juice into gelatin. Set aside 2 cups of gelatin mixture; keep at room temperature. Chill remaining gelatin until syrupy. Fold cherries, celery and walnuts into syrupy gelatin. Pour into 6-1/2-cup ring mold. Chill until almost firm. (Mixture should appear to be set but feel sticky to the touch. It should also flow slightly when tipped to one side.) Gradually add reserved gelatin to softened cream cheese, beating until smooth. Stir in applesauce. Spoon cream cheese mixture over cherry mixture in mold. Chill until firm. Unmold onto lettuce-lined serving dish. Serve with mayonnaise or salad dressing sprinkled with additional walnuts if desired. Serves 10 to 12.
—Blanche Niemann, Lake Benton, Minnesota

JUICE: *After draining fruits for a recipe, freeze any leftover juice. Use it for gelatin recipes in place of part of the water.*

CHERRY DESSERT SALAD

Salad:
1/4 cup sugar
1 envelope unflavored gelatin
1/8 teaspoon salt
1 cup boiling water
1 teaspoon lemon juice
1/4 cup mayonnaise or salad
dressing

1 8-ounce package cream cheese
softened
1 20-ounce can tart, pitted, red
cherries, drained, reserving
juice
1 3-ounce package cherry gelatin
1/4 cup sugar
1 cup orange juice

Lemon sauce:
1/4 cup sugar
1 tablespoon cornstarch
1 cup water

2 tablespoons butter
1/2 teaspoon lemon peel, grated
1 tablespoon lemon juice

Salad: Combine sugar, unflavored gelatin and salt; mix well. Add boiling water, stirring to dissolve gelatin and sugar. Add lemon juice, mayonnaise and cream cheese, beating until smooth. Pour into lightly greased mold. Chill until almost firm. Meanwhile, place cherry juice in small saucepan with cherry gelatin, sugar and orange juice. Heat, stirring, to dissolve gelatin. Cool until syrupy. Fold in cherries; pour over cream cheese mixture in mold. Chill until set. **Sauce:** Combine sugar, cornstarch and water, cooking and stirring over low heat. When thickened, remove from heat. Stir in butter, lemon peel and lemon juice. Chill. Unmold salad onto lettuce. Spoon sauce over top.   **—Gladys Getschman, Baraboo, Wisconsin**

Inaugural Salads

CHEERY CHERRY SALAD

1 3-ounce package raspberry
gelatin
2 cups water, divided
1 21-ounce can cherry pie filling
1 3-ounce package lemon gelatin
1 3-ounce package cream cheese

1/3 cup mayonnaise or salad
dressing
1 8-1/4-ounce can crushed
pineapple, undrained
1/2 cup whipping cream
1 cup miniature marshmallows
Chopped nuts

Dissolve raspberry gelatin in 1 cup boiling water. Stir in cherry pie filling. Pour into 9-in. square pan. Chill until firm. Dissolve lemon gelatin in 1 cup boiling water. Beat together cream cheese and mayonnaise. Gradually add lemon gelatin. Stir in undrained pineapple. Whip cream; fold into lemon mixture. Add marshmallows. Spread over cherry layer. Chill until set. Top with chopped nuts. **Note:** To make Cheery Cherry Dessert, top with whipped cream instead of nuts. Serves 12.
                              —Mrs. Don Sanderson, Holland, Manitoba

BERRY FIZZ SALAD

1 16-ounce can pitted, dark, sweet cherries, drained, reserving juice
1 20-ounce can crushed pineapple, drained, reserving juice
2 cups reserved fruit juices
1 3-ounce package black cherry gelatin
1 3-ounce package raspberry gelatin
1 12-ounce can cola beverage, chilled
1 cup diced celery
1 cup chopped pecans
1/2 cup flaked coconut
1 6-ounce package cream cheese, softened

Bring fruit juices to boil. Add gelatin; stir well. Stir in cola. Chill until slightly thickened. Combine celery, pecans, cherries, pineapple and coconut. Beat cream cheese until smooth and fluffy. Beat into gelatin mixture until well blended. Stir in fruit mixture. Pour into 13- x 9-in. pan. Chill. Cut into 16 squares. Serve on lettuce, topped with whipped cream and chopped nuts if desired.   **—Cynthia Kannenberg, Brown Deer, Wisconsin**

BING CHERRY REFRIGERATOR SALAD

2 eggs, well beaten
2 tablespoons sugar
6 tablespoons lemon juice
1/8 teaspoon salt
1/4 cup butter, melted
2 cups miniature marshmallows
1 20-ounce can pineapple chunks, drained
1 cup chopped nuts
1 20-ounce can bing cherries, drained and halved
1 cup whipping cream, whipped

Combine beaten eggs, sugar, lemon juice and salt in top of double boiler. Cook over boiling water until mixture thickens, stirring constantly. Remove from heat; add butter and marshmallows. Stir until marshmallows are almost melted. Cool. When mixture begins to thicken, fold in pineapple, nuts, cherries and whipped cream. Spoon into individual serving dishes or glass salad bowl. Chill.   **—Marlene Konrad, Tripp, South Dakota**

CHERRY DELIGHT SALAD

4 egg yolks, beaten
1/3 cup sugar
1 lemon rind, grated
Juice of 2 lemons
1 pint whipping cream, whipped
1 16-ounce can bing cherries, drained
1 20-ounce can crushed pineapple, drained
5 cups miniature marshmallows
1 cup chopped walnuts

Cook beaten egg yolks, sugar, lemon rind and juice in double boiler until thickened. Cool; fold in whipped cream. Add fruits, marshmallows and nuts. Pour into 13- x 9-in. pan; chill 24 hours. Cut into squares to serve.
—Izetta Tasler, Atkinson, Nebraska

MACARONI FRUIT SALAD

4 eggs, beaten
1 8-1/4-ounce can crushed
  pineapple, drained, reserving
  juice
1/2 cup sugar
1/4 cup lemon juice
1-1/2 cups ring or small-shell
  macaroni, cooked

1/2 pint heavy cream, whipped
3 cups diced apples
1 cup miniature marshmallows
1 cup coconut
1 cup chopped pecans
1 16-ounce can pitted, dark,
  sweet cherries, drained or 2
  cups fresh

Combine eggs, pineapple juice, sugar and lemon in saucepan. Cook over low heat, stirring, until mixture thickens; cool slightly. Fold into cooked macaroni. Cover; chill several hours. Fold in drained pineapple, whipped cream, apples, marshmallows, coconut and nuts; chill. Just before serving, fold in halved cherries. Serve on lettuce, topped with cherries and chopped nuts if desired. —**Dorothy D. Davis, Yulee, Florida**

FROSTED CHERRY SALAD

1 16-ounce can pitted, tart, red
  cherries, undrained
1/3 cup sugar
1 3-ounce package cherry gelatin
3/4 cup cold water

2/3 cup chopped celery
1/3 cup sliced, stuffed olives
1 3-ounce package cream cheese,
  softened
2 tablespoons mayonnaise
1/4 cup chopped pecans or walnuts

Combine cherries, juice, sugar and gelatin in saucepan. Heat, stirring, until gelatin is dissolved. Add cold water; chill until mixture begins to thicken. Add celery and olives. Pour into 8-in. square pan. Chill. Blend softened cream cheese with mayonnaise. Spread over top of gelatin mixture. Sprinkle with chopped nuts. Chill until ready to serve. Cut into squares. Serve on salad greens. Serves 6. —**Joyce Diehl, Maple Park, Illinois**

CHARMING CHERRY FRUIT SALAD

1 cup cream cheese, softened
1/8 teaspoon salt
1 cup crushed pineapple, drained
1 cup pitted bing cherries,
  drained

1 cup diced peaches, drained
1 cup mandarin orange segments,
  drained
1/2 cup mayonnaise
1 pint whipping cream, whipped

Combine cheese, salt and drained fruits. Chill. Fold mayonnaise into whipped cream. Blend into cheese mixture. Place in ice cube tray. Freeze. To serve, cut into smaller cubes and place on lettuce-lined plates. Garnish with whipped cream and cherries if desired. Serves 8.
—**Cynthia Kannenberg, Brown Deer, Wisconsin**

CHERRY-CHICKEN SALAD

Salad:

1 cup pitted, halved, sweet
  cherries, fresh or canned
  (drained)
2 cups chicken, cooked, cubed

1/2 cup diced celery
1/2 cup pineapple tidbits, drained
1/4 cup sliced, blanched almonds
Salad greens

Dressing:

1/2 cup mayonnaise
1/4 cup sour cream

1/8 teaspoon horseradish
1/4 teaspoon salt

Salad: Mix cherries, chicken, celery, pineapple and almonds. Place in bowl lined with salad greens. **Dressing:** Combine mayonnaise, sour cream, horseradish and salt. Mix well. Toss lightly into salad. Garnish with more cherries if desired. Serve chilled. Serves 6.

—**Blanche Niemann, Lake Benton, Minnesota**

FROZEN CHERRY SALAD LOAF

1 16-ounce can pitted, dark,
  sweet cherries, drained
1 11-ounce can mandarin
  oranges, drained
1 8-ounce package cream cheese,
  softened
1 cup dairy sour cream

1/4 cup sugar
1/4 teaspoon salt
1 8-1/4-ounce can crushed
  pineapple, drained
2 cups miniature marshmallows
1/2 cup chopped pecans

Reserve a few cherries and orange sections for garnish. Beat softened cream cheese until fluffy; blend in sour cream, sugar and salt. Fold in fruits, marshmallows and nuts. Pour into 8-1/2- x 4-1/2-in. loaf pan. Freeze 6 hours or overnight. Unmold; garnish with orange sections and cherries. Serves 8.

—**Dorothy D. Davis, Yulee, Florida**

CHERRY CREAM SALAD

21-ounce can cherry pie filling
10-1/2-ounce bag miniature
marshmallows

1 30-ounce can fruit cocktail,
  drained
1 cup whipping cream, whipped

Mix together cherry pie filling, marshmallows and fruit cocktail. Fold in whipped cream. Chill. Add coconut and chopped nuts if desired.

—**Myrtle Barber, Ladysmith, Wisconsin**

PIZZA PARTY. *Why not have a pizza party featuring your favorite cheese or sausage pizza and a cherry dessert that looks like pizza but tastes like pie? (See our Cherry Pizza recipe, page 8.)*

Index

For More Good Country Cooking...

MICROWAVE TREATS. You can surprise your family with an extra-special dessert or sweet snack even on a busy day. Just use one of the quick-to-make, great-to-eat recipes in *Microwave Treats!* Choose from pies, cakes, baked squares, cobblers, puddings and more. Just $3.95.

AWARD-WINNING RECIPES. This book includes the *best*—4 years of *Farm Wife News* recipe contest winners, runners-up and featured favorites! You'll find the top recipes we received for appetizers, side dishes, main dishes and desserts, plus special chapters on cooking in the microwave and making jams and jellies. Just $3.95.

COOKIE JAR COOKBOOK. When hands reach into the cookie jar at your house, they'll like finding the extra-special cookies made from the unique recipes in this book. There are oatmeal, chocolate chip, butter, peanut butter or spice cookies...or coconut, chocolate, fruit, honey, nut and even fancier "novelty" cookies! Only $3.95.

MICROWAVE MAGIC. This cookbook is filled cover-to-cover with great microwave recipes for meat, fish and poultry dishes...potatoes, rice and vegetables...plus rolls and muffins to go with any dinner. *Microwave Magic* is a *must* for any cook who owns a microwave. It also includes recipes for quick soup-and-sandwich suppers, hors d'oeuvres, desserts, cookies, candies and more, plus great "microwave tips" from rural cooks who learned by trial and error. Just $3.95.

CHOCOLATE LOVERS' COOKBOOK. Pies, cakes, refrigerator and freezer desserts, cookies and squares, candies and other chocolate treats make this cookbook a "chocoholic's" delight! Instead of giving a box of chocolate candy on the next special occasion, why not put a ribbon around this *Chocolate Lovers' Cookbook?* Just $3.95.

To order these books or extra copies of *Cherry Delights,* please send $3.95 per copy—plus 75¢ for postage and handling—to Country Store, P.O. Box 572, Milwaukee, WI 53201. (For orders of more than 1 book, please enclose 75¢ postage for the first book plus 25¢ more for each additional book.)